PORT WASHINGTON CHILDREN'S CENTER
LANDMARK SQUARE
232 MAIN STREET, SUITE 2
PORT WASHINGTON, N.Y. 11050-3224

The Magic of Micah Lasher

More Than Fifty Tricks
That Will Amaze and Delight
Everyone—Including You

Micah Lasher

Illustrated by Akemi Yoshida

A Fireside Book
Published by Simon & Schuster

FIRESIDE
Rockefeller Center
1230 Avenue of the Americas
New York, NY 10020

FIRESIDE and colophon are registered trademarks
of Simon & Schuster Inc.

Designed by Richard Oriolo

Manufactured in the United States of America

1 3 5 7 9 10 8 6 4 2

Library of Congress Cataloging-in-Publication Data

Lasher, Micah.
The magic of Micah Lasher : more than fifty tricks that will amaze
and delight everyone, including you / Micah Lasher.
p.   cm.
"A Fireside book."
Includes bibliographical references.
ISBN 0-684-81390-4
1. Conjuring.   2. Tricks.   I. Title.
GV1547.L29   1996
793.8—dc20   96-26052
                                                         CIP

ISBN 0-684-81390-4

For Risa and Renee,
the two best sisters (and spectators)
in the whole world

$\mathscr{A}$cknowledgments

I'd like to thank the following people:

Akemi Yoshida, for 210 beautiful illustrations, a huge contribution to this book. Akemi was great to work with. She seemed to do those drawings at warp speed, all the more astonishing because of their incredibly high clarity and simplicity.

My two literary agents (also my aunt and uncle), Maureen and Eric Lasher. Not only were they always there with support, they were the ones who came up with the idea to write the book in the first place!

My editor, Betsy Radin, for her encouragement, and understanding that school had to come first (most of the time).

Matthew Walker, her assistant, who did a ton of work for this book, and who kept me advised every step of the way.

My two historical researchers, Joel Stein and Ben Robinson. Joel's research was his first real trip into the world of magic, and he did a really great job. Ben, magician and magic historian, came up with anecdotes no one else could have found.

Sue Oskam, for transcribing all of the interviews. Even those that she received on a Monday when I needed the transcripts on Tuesday!

Finally, my parents, Stephanie and Albert Lasher, and my sisters, Risa and Renee, for continuous support and their cheerful willingness to act as either spectators or students as I tested and refined each of the tricks in the book. They also read through the book a number of times, looking for errors and unclear illustrations. This thanks is extended especially to my father, who spent many hours, often late into the night, helping me with this project.

Other people who helped with this book include Marilyn Abraham, former vice president of Simon and Schuster, for helping get the idea off the ground; Lisa Cox, an understanding stranger who went out of her way to help me reach General H. Norman Schwarzkopf; Myron Kandel, a family friend and distinguished journalist who also was a great help in my attempts to reach interview subjects; Molly O'Neill, whose large *New York Times* article on magic created a snowball effect of success for me and helped lead to my writing this book; my friend Jake Katz, who helped me proofread part of the book on a bus trip to Boston; all my interview subjects, who, as you will see, comprise a large portion of this book, and were most generous with their time; and finally, all the teachers I've ever had. There is an NBC "The More You Know" segment that sums up my feelings toward teachers. In the spot, actor Jonathan Silverman says, "Knowledge is power, and teachers are just giving the stuff away. Pretty generous, huh?" Thank you all very much.

I thank David Fattel for really getting me started in magic. My thanks also to other magician friends for sharing their knowledge with me. They include Andrew West; Bob McAllister; Jed Smith; Jason Litwak; Robb Weinstock; John Alban; Lenny Greenfader; Marvin Steiner; David Blair; Gene Maze; Meir Yedid; Harry Lorayne; David Goodsell; John Blake; Tony Spina; David Oliver; the New York City magic fraternity; my fellow members of Assembly 25 of the Society of American Magicians, especially Herb Zarrow, Ron Wohl, Mel Fields, and Adrian Kuiper; and many other marvelous magicians who made it possible for a kid like me to experience the joy of magic.

I am indebted to you all.

ontents

I

A Brief Introduction to Magic

II

The Tricks

Preface

he art of magic has a time-honored and distinguished history. The word *magic* itself probably came from one of the languages developed in ancient Middle Eastern civilization, perhaps by the Persians or the Chaldeans. It was the word for priest, *imga*. It soon became *maga* when it entered the Assyrian language and, finally, *magus* in Latin.

Few hobbies attract as diverse a crowd as does magic. Magicians are people of all types, famous and not so famous. There are young magicians, which I am, and older magicians, such as Meyer Lang, who at age eighty-seven and still an active performer was honored in 1994 by the Society of American Magicians' (SAM) Parent Assembly as Magician of the Year. There are rich magicians and poor magicians, tall magicians and short magicians, people of many different ethnic backgrounds and many different occupations. Magic is a meritocracy. In the world of magic, what counts is not who you are, or how famous you are, but how well you perform as a magician.

Here are some observations and notes that I hope you will find useful in your journey into the wonderful world of magic.

1. The purpose of this book, primarily, is to teach you to perform magic. It is also designed to educate you in the history of this craft and introduce some of the most important figures in the development of magic as an art.

2. It is, essentially, a beginner's book. However, the tricks range from those that are self-working and do not involve sleight of hand to more advanced tricks that do. All the tricks will require at least some practice before you are ready to perform them.

3. Every chapter (i.e., "Card Magic," "Coin and Currency Magic") is organized with the easiest and less technically demanding tricks first, followed by those requiring more practice.

4. Sleights, for the most part, are described in detail immediately following the first trick in which they are used. After that, they are simply referred to. You can look them up in the index. In the index, the first reference will be to the description of the sleight.

5. There is a great amount of literature on magic, going back to *The Discouerie of Witchcrafte,* by Reginald Scot, published in 1584. The tricks in this book were carefully selected based on ease of preparation and high audience impact.

6. Only two of the tricks in this book require props that wouldn't normally be found around the house. The props needed for the two tricks, the "Cups and Balls," and the "Sponge Balls," which are listed in the text, can be bought at any magic shop. There are magic shops throughout the United States and in major cities around the world, most of which sell via mail order as well as over the counter (see the list of shops in the United States in the back of the book).

7. When following the directions for the tricks in this book, when references are made to right or left (e.g., "right side of the deck" or "move

the deck to the right") it means the magician's right or the magician's left. All such performance directions are from the magician's point of view. In addition, when I refer to the front or back (mostly in references like "the front side of the deck") the front is the side closest to the audience, and the back is the side closest to the performer.

A Note, Especially for Women

In the initial draft of this book I used gender-neutral language. In an effort to be responsive to the sensitivities of readers, every gender-specific pronoun was written in he/she form. Midway through the task, I concluded this was annoying for the writer and, as friends and other early readers advised, annoying and obtrusive to the reader as well.

The decision to use the masculine form was based on the fact that more than 90 percent of magicians are male. It was in no way a chauvinistic decision. It is my sincere wish that this book will help increase the number of female magicians.

Today there are more magicians in the world than ever before. Some of them belong to magic clubs that meet regularly. The two major international magic organizations, the Society of American Magicians and the International Brotherhood of Magicians, have over twenty thousand members and are growing at a steady rate. Their memberships include lawyers, doctors, mathematicians, entrepreneurs, clergymen, and people from all walks of life who use magic to enrich their lives.

A Note, Especially for Southpaws

 agic books are almost universally written for righties. This is because not only are the large majority of magicians right-handed but the large majority of the population, as well. All the tricks described in this book are written as a righty would do them; all the illustrations are of a right-handed person doing the tricks. However, it is not that difficult to translate this book into southpaw language. Wherever you see the word "right," make it "left," and vice versa. Mentally reverse all the illustrations. This may sound difficult, but many of my friends in magic are lefties, and they tell me it is easy.

**The most beautiful
thing we can experience
is the mysterious. It is
the source of all true art
and science.**

—ALBERT EINSTEIN

A Brief

Introduction to

Magic

The Performance of Magic

he presentation of a trick is basically what you say and how you act during its performance. You know your presentation has been a success when you see a child burst into laughter or someone's eyes widen in amazement. Now, if you choose, you could just talk through the trick. "Pick a card . . . I'm going to take out the two aces . . . They're going to locate your card . . . There it is, between the two aces!" This form of presentation may puzzle and even surprise, but it lacks enchantment, does not produce a sense of wonder, and hardly defies the laws of nature. In the minds of the spectators, whether they can articulate it or not, they have seen little more than a technician displaying his skill. You can be the most technically talented magician in the world, but all of that means nothing if your work is received with yawns.

Great Teachers of Magic

*T*here would be far fewer magicians if none were willing to share their knowledge of the art of magic. In the history of magic, there have been outstanding teachers. The late Tony Slydini, a legend for his extraordinary sense of misdirection, was also a professional magic teacher and, during his long life, had many students. Harry Lorayne, card magician and premier memory expert, has probably written more books filled with his own material than anyone else. He also has produced instructional videos on his magic and is editor and publisher of a highly regarded monthly publication for close-up magicians, *Apocalypse*. Jean Hugard wrote some of the most important works on card magic, many of which are used as prime references. He completed the manuscript of *Greater Magic* upon the death of its creator and author, John Northern Hilliard. Hugard for many years also edited an important monthly magic magazine, *Hugard's Magic Monthly*. Harlan Tarbell was the author of *The Tarbell Course in Magic*, originally a correspondence course that became a set of six books that covered everything from beginning to advanced magic and is still required reading for any magician. Actually, Tarbell was originally only going to illustrate the course. However, when the author did not deliver, Tarbell took on the task of writing it as well. Richard Kaufman, half of the publishing team of Kaufman & Greenberg, has written, coauthored, or edited more than forty-four books since the firm's founding in 1977.

John Cassidy and Michael Stroud sum up this point beautifully in *The Klutz Book of Magic.* "Magic is not done, it's *performed*. Like any performance art, it withers away to nothing if it's not presented in the grand style. Moving your feet around is not dancing, reading the lyrics is not singing, and pulling a rabbit out of a hat is not magic."

This is not to say that a high skill level in and of itself cannot entertain. Watching a potter shape a vase out of a lump of clay can be transfixing. The magician, however, through presentation, has a larger opportunity; he has the ability to lift the art of magic to a level beyond skill alone. That's what makes it magic.

Enhancing a trick through creative presentation adds value. The presentation may not be any more complex than a simple story. For instance, in the example above involving the aces finding a selected card, the aces can be "ace" detectives and the selected card an arch criminal. This is a theme that I use regularly in my performances, including some on the *Today* show and other TV venues in which I have been invited to perform.

One important thing about using stories in magic is that you should tell a story *with* a trick, NOT a story *and* a trick. However, fusing a good magic trick with an intriguing story is not the only type of presentation. Humor is another. Making magic funny can work for some people, but be careful not to offend your audience with tasteless comedy. Also, if you are performing as a magician and not as a comedian, it is important to strike a balance. The comedy supplements the magic, not the reverse. A cautionary note: some people do not have a personality that lends itself to humor. If you are one of them, don't force it on yourself and on your audience.

A friend, Jason Litwak, is currently preparing a magic act that has one theme, the movie *The Blues Brothers.* Every trick is connected in some way to that movie. He does a coin trick, but instead of using coins, he uses miniature harmonicas. He makes a selected card float out of the type of hat worn by Dan Ackroyd and John Belushi in the movie. For the climax, he is planning to produce an electric guitar. How did he arrive at this theme? He simply loves the movie.

Whatever story you tell, music you use, or theme you choose, it must fit your personality. If you find a story that will work with the trick but you don't like telling it, DON'T USE IT. You must put as much time and thought into creating an effective presentation as you do in practicing the magic technique required for the trick. If you have good presentation that fits your personality, the entertainment value of your magic will be greatly enhanced. An effective presentation will give great pleasure to your audience and will enhance the joy of being a magician.

Magicians believe that magic is a great hobby. It's fun. Magic also teaches grace, self-confidence, social skills, and manual dexterity, and it gives you tools you can use in everyday life. Magic requires determination and stick-to-itiveness, time, and effort. And in the end, there is nothing more satisfying to a magician than the feeling of knowing he has enchanted his audience.

The Lion's Paw

Ousman Sallah is a former foreign minister of the Gambia, a small country on the west coast of Africa. For a time, he was ambassador to the United States. Sallah recalls that as a young man, he had seen a tribal medicine man turn his forearm into a lion's paw and then back again to human form. My father, an old friend of Sallah's, was skeptical. Sallah said, "Albert, if I wrote to my mother and told her I had seen a bear ride a bicycle around an arena with twenty thousand people looking on, she would think I was crazy. I saw the medicine man change his arm to a lion's paw."

The Magician's Ten Commandments

1. NEVER TELL HOW IT'S DONE. When you do a magic trick, don't tell how the trick works. It diminishes the art and destroys the mystery. In revealing the secret, you remove the enchantment from your performance and most of the joy as well. Suddenly it isn't magical anymore. If you think about it, it's unfair to your audience. The person who presses you to find out how it works probably doesn't have any interest in being able to do the trick. He just wants to satisfy his curiosity. When people ask me how I do a trick, I suggest they go to the library and take out a book on magic. If they are willing to do this, chances are they are actually interested in learning to do magic.

★

2. NEVER DO THE SAME TRICK TWICE. Many tricks depend on the principles of misdirection (see Commandment 7). Doing the same trick twice makes it harder to distract the audience the second time around. Also, when an audience sees the exact same thing twice, they will lose interest. You are, in effect, challenging your audience. You're saying, "You see, I can even do it again and you still can't figure it out." This moves your trick from an entertainment to a challenge. This will inspire heckling and will generally annoy your audience.

★

3. NEVER DETRACT FROM ANOTHER MAGICIAN'S PERFORMANCE. Never tell anyone how another magician does his tricks, never sabotage another magician's performance, and never heckle another magician. Julian Stanley is an experienced street magician who can be found most weekends performing near the entrance to New York's Central Park Zoo. Once, in the course of his masterful sponge ball routine, he asked the audience, "How many sponge balls do I have in my hand?" Though the spectators had seen him put three in his hand, he had actually put in only one. While everyone else in the audience said three, one young man in his twenties yelled out, "Just one!" The audience quieted. Stanley said, "Oh, you've seen me do this trick before." The young man responded, "No, I do magic." A smile came to Stanley's face, as he slowly said, "Well, if you were a true magician, you would know not to embarrass another." Stanley went on with his performance, and the heckler quickly left. Although Stanley handled the incident well, he should not have had to deal with it. If you break this rule, you not only diminish the art of magic but specifically diminish and hurt another magician.

★

4. PRACTICE, PRACTICE, PRACTICE. Always practice before you perform. If you perform a trick before you are ready, you might accidentally expose its modus operandi. Even if you don't expose the secret, your confidence will fade, your performance will not be as smooth, and your audience will not be as entertained as they might be. It is always worth taking a little extra time to be able to do the trick perfectly. Generally, I practice in front of a mirror. This enables me to see the trick almost as the audience would, make sure sight angles are right, and check for revealing "flashes." I will then present the trick, more than once, to close friends, family members, or other magicians and check their reactions. This helps me polish the trick to perfection.

★

5. RESPECT YOUR AUDIENCE. Always treat your audience respectfully. If you follow this rule, they just might return the favor. Either way, your job is to entertain your audience, not to offend them.

★

6. BE NATURAL. Remember, the hand is NOT quicker than the eye. Any quick or odd motion will detract from the magical effect you are trying to achieve. The audience will know you are engaging in some form of trickery. Harry Lorayne, who in the contemporary world of magic is widely considered to be a magician's magician, says in his book, *Close-Up Card Magic,* "If the audience knows something was done, it is as bad as if they know *what* was done."

★

7. USE MISDIRECTION WHENEVER POSSIBLE. One concept mentioned in almost every teaching text on magic is misdirection. It is the magician's word for distraction. It means drawing people's attention to one thing while you secretly do another. Even if you can do a sleight perfectly, it is safer if the spectators aren't looking when and where the sleight is taking place. If they're not looking, they can't see! That is the premise behind misdirection. Commandments 8 and 9 are the two cardinal rules of misdirection.

★

8. USE A BIGGER MOTION TO COVER A SMALLER ONE. If you move your left hand in a large, sweeping motion and secretly reposition a hidden coin in your right hand, a small motion, the audience will follow the sweep of your left hand. Another example might involve a deck of cards. Let's say you have palmed a card with your left hand. One way to misdirect the audience's attention would be to move the deck, with your right hand, to the front of the table, asking a spectator to shuffle and cut it. All eyes will be on the spectator, and you will be free to do what you wish with the palmed card.

★

9. LOOK INTO THE SPECTATORS' EYES. They will in turn look into yours. This also works with an audience. Make eye contact with as many people as possible. They will make eye contact with you, as will the entire audience, helping distract from the secret action you may be undertaking at the time. Corollary to this rule is that at all times you should endeavor to follow the eyes of the spectator. If you notice the spectator briefly looking away, take advantage of that opportunity. When performing in front of an audience, focus on the eyes of one or two very watchful spectators. If they aren't looking where the action is going to take place, the likelihood is that no one else is either.

★

10. HAVE FUN. Magic is fun to learn and fun to do. I imagine this is why you are interested in magic. Lawyer/magician Peter Kougasian says, "I have always found it unbelievably enjoyable to perform magic. And most of the time, if the magician is really enjoying a performance, the audience is, too."

Tools of the Trade

he tools or props you use in performing magic can make or break your performance. Below is a brief description of what you will need to perform the tricks in this book.

1. **Card Magic:** This one should be pretty obvious—a deck of cards. However, there are quite a few variables in decks of cards. First and foremost, you will want a deck that has a white border on its back. Usually this border is a little less than a quarter of an inch. If the deck you use doesn't have a border, you will not be able to perform tricks like "Triumph," "Sandwich, Please," and others.

   In addition to the border, you will want a deck that has a smooth finish, preferably an "air-cushion finish." This will enable you to spread the cards easily. I would suggest Bicycle brand.

Finally, there is an issue of size. There are two main sizes of cards—poker and bridge. Bridge-size cards are slightly narrower than poker-size cards. If you practice with bridge-size cards and then are presented with a poker-size deck (which is by far the more common of the two), you may have some difficulty because the cards are larger. But if you learn to manipulate the poker-size cards, manipulating the bridge-size cards will be even easier. So the bottom line is that I suggest Bicycle poker-size playing cards.

2. **Coin and Currency Magic:** For these tricks I suggest going to a coin shop and getting five half-dollars. Five is the most you will need in any of the routines. In addition, I would advise spending a few extra dollars and getting *silver* half-dollars, rather than the current coins that are constructed from a combination of metals. The silver coins have a nicer, shinier look to them and have a good sound when they clink against each other. Kennedy half-dollars were made of silver in 1964, and those are beautiful. If the shop doesn't have those, Franklin half-dollars (which, incidentally, are the coins I use) will serve wonderfully well.

   If you have tiny, tiny hands (and they would have to be quite tiny; I have been using half-dollars since age ten), you might try using Susan B. Anthony dollars. These coins are slightly larger than a regular quarter but smaller than half-dollars. And if your mitts are huge, you might try silver dollars. These are quite a bit larger than half-dollars, but work well for some people.

3. **Ball Magic:** The descriptions of the routines later in the book detail all the props you will need.

4. **Kitchen-Table Magic:** The props vary for each trick and are described in the text.

5. **Mental Magic:** Again, the props vary for each trick and are described in the text.

6. **Rope Magic:** For rope tricks, you might use soft clothesline, though I suggest investing a few dollars in a hank of magician's rope. This is rope that is specially made for magicians and can most probably be bought at your local magic shop.

7. Accessories: An accessory that many close-up magicians consider important is a close-up pad or mat. It has a cushiony, feltlike surface and a rubberized bottom. The bottom provides enough friction to serve as an anchor, and the surface makes some routines easier to do. The close-up pad will guarantee a clean and smooth performing surface and will protect tabletops from scratches. The sizes vary. I use a 12" x 15" size, which costs about $13.

III

The Tricks

Card Magic

o one knows how or exactly when playing cards originated. Records in the British Museum point to Italy or France in the fifteenth century as their origin. The first deck engraved with an artistic design was said to have been created by a man who is known only as "The Master of Playing Cards" from Basel, Switzerland. His first deck was made sometime around A.D. 1445 and is represented by one remaining card, the Queen of Cyclamen. This artifact can be seen in the Museum of Fine Arts in Boston. The depiction of the Queen on this card resembles, in some respects, religious madonnas.

By A.D. 1500 playing cards had become popular in Europe, though they were still too expensive for wandering entertainers. A picture of people playing with cards is shown in a German book, *Das Guildian Spiel,* printed in Augsburg in 1472.

Famous Americans

Some of the most famous Americans are also magicians. Former president George Bush, while still in office, often visited Al's Magic Shop in Washington, D.C., to pick up the latest tricks and watch proprietor Al Cohen demonstrate them. Notre Dame football coach Lou Holtz dazzles his colleagues with one of his favorite tricks, the Torn and Restored newspaper. Neil Patrick Harris of TV's *Doogie Howser* stops by Tannen's Magic whenever he's in New York. General H. Norman Schwarzkopf, member in good standing of the International Brotherhood of Magicians, is said to have entertained himself by practicing magic to relieve some of the tensions of the Persian Gulf War.

Playing cards from the fifteenth to eighteenth centuries were a little different from today's standard deck of fifty-two cards. The fifty-two-card deck probably derived from the tarot deck. The tarot deck consisted of four suits, each having fourteen numbered cards, and an additional twenty-two cards, which were pictorial. Tarot cards are still commonly used as aids in telling individual fortunes and predicting the future.

Cards were used as a calendar during the European Renaissance. The suits identified the four seasons. Each of fifty-two weeks was represented by a card, the court cards representing periods of tax collection by the royalty.

The earliest record of a magician using playing cards is in a story about Chevalier Giovanni Guiseppe Pinetti in the 1780s. A French book, *La magie blanche devoillee* (White magic unveiled), pictures him performing one of his favorite tricks. He would burn a chosen playing card and stuff the ashes into a gun barrel. Pinetti would then fire at the wall of the stage, where the card would reappear, restored.

The Viennese "Beethoven of Magic," Johann Nepomuk Hofzinser (1806–75), is regarded as the pioneer and founder of close-up card magic. Hofzinser referred to card conjuring as "the poetry of magic."

The main reason for the popularity of cards among magicians is their extraordinary versatility. A deck of cards may be the only prop in a magician's arsenal that enables him to perform all twelve of the basic effects of magic: production, vanish, transposition, transformation, animation, penetration, levitation, sympathetic reaction, time control, escape, mentalism, and invulnerability.

Twenty-one

E F F E C T

The deck is shuffled. Three piles of cards, each containing seven cards, are placed face down on the table. A spectator selects one of the packets. He is instructed to file through the cards in the chosen packet, taking care not to let anyone else see them, and mentally select and memorize one of them.

The cards are then collected into a single packet and redealt, face down, into three equal piles. As he deals, the magician shows each card to the spectator. The spectator then indicates which pile contains his card. The process is repeated a second time.

The magician then scatters the cards, still face down, across the table. He ends up with one card under his hand. That card is found to be the one mentally selected by the spectator.

M E T H O D

STEP 1: Shuffle the deck. If you wish, have the spectator do it.

★

STEP 2: Have the spectator deal three piles of seven cards each, face down, on to the table.

★

STEP 3: Have the spectator select one of the piles.

★

STEP 4: Instruct him to file through the cards, mentally selecting and memorizing one of them. Caution the spectator to take care that nobody else sees the cards.

★

STEP 5: Have the spectator place his packet of seven cards on top of any one of the two packets remaining on the table.

★

STEP 6: Have him take the remaining packet of seven cards and place it on top of the double pile of fourteen cards. The packet the spectator looked through is now sandwiched between the other two packets.

N O T E

★

This trick was a favorite of the silent film comedian Harold Lloyd, himself an amateur magician. It falls into the category of self-working card tricks, tricks that require no sleight of hand. These effects can have as powerful an impact as those that do use sleight of hand. This particular self-working trick is one that falls into the mathematical category. Alan Ackerman, a math professor at the University of Nevada at Las Vegas, often will show his class a mathematical card trick and give extra credit to the student who first works out its mathematics.

Harry Houdini

*H*arry Houdini (1874–1926) may be the most famous magician of all time, second only to the mythical Merlin. Though Houdini was best known for his incredible escape artistry, he was a fine magician in many different areas and actually started out as "The King of Cards." Houdini's name at birth was Ehrich Weiss. He borrowed the name Houdini from the famous French magician Jean Eugene Robert-Houdin and chose Harry in honor of the great American magician Harry Kellar. Houdini spent a great deal of his time debunking fake psychics and clairvoyants. One of Houdini's most important roles in magic was his nine-year term as president, starting in 1917, of the Society of American Magicians. The SAM now has thousands of members in chapters throughout the world, many of which were organized during Houdini's term. The movie *Houdini,* starring Tony Curtis, is responsible for the misconception that Houdini accidentally drowned while performing one of his escapes. His death is normally attributed to his habit of challenging spectators to punch him in the stomach. Houdini took pride in his powerful physique, including an especially strong abdomen. In Montreal, on October 22, 1926, Houdini was in his dressing room, lying on his couch, reading his mail. A visiting McGill University student asked if it was true that Houdini was able to take a punch in the stomach. Houdini murmured affirmatively. The student proceeded to punch him a number of times on the right side of his abdomen. Ten days later, he died of peritonitis, resulting from a ruptured appendix. Although many biographers link the incident in the Montreal dressing room to his death, there

★

STEP 7: Pick up the pile of twenty-one cards and redeal them face down on to the table, starting with the first three cards placed side by side. The next three cards are similarly dealt out, side by side on top of the first three, and so on, until the packet of twenty-one cards is exhausted. You now have, once again, three piles of seven cards each.

As each card is dealt, show its face to the spectator and ask him to remember which of the piles includes the selected card (fig. 1). Caution him not to react in any way when he sees the selected card.

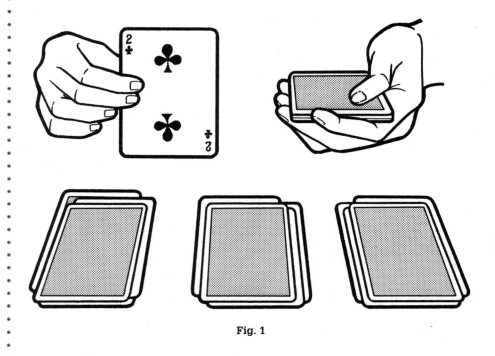

Fig. 1

★

STEP 8: Ask the spectator to point to the pile containing the selected card.

★

STEP 9: Place the pile with the spectator's card on top of either of the two other piles.

★

STEP 10: Place the last pile of seven cards on top of the pile of fourteen cards. Once again, the spectator's packet is sandwiched between the other two packets.

★

STEP 11: Repeat steps 7–10.

★

STEP 12: At this point, the spectator's card will be the eleventh card from the top of the pile of twenty-one cards.

★

STEP 13: Deal the cards, face down, randomly on to the table. Be sure to count the cards silently as you go so you can identify the eleventh card and note where on the table you tossed it.

★

STEP 14: Place the hand closest to the eleventh card flat on top of it. The spectator should have no knowledge of the significance of the placement of your hand. Place your other hand somewhere else, anywhere, on top of the scattered cards (fig. 2). Move both hands about, randomly,

Fig. 2

mixing and scattering the cards, but be sure to keep the eleventh card under your hand throughout the process. Stop mixing the cards around and pause for a moment. Now slide the hand with the selected card out and away from the scattered mess of cards. Be sure to keep the selected

is no known medical connection between blows to the abdomen and a ruptured appendix. Each year, on the anniversary of his death, a graveside memorial service, the "Broken Wand" ceremony, is conducted by the Society of American Magicians.

Fig. 3

card under the hand (fig. 3). It should look as if you randomly picked it from among the scattered cards.

STEP 15: Ask the spectator to name the card he mentally selected. Turn over the eleventh card, the very card named by the spectator.

You Do as I Do

EFFECT

Two decks are used, a red one and a blue one. One is selected by a spectator, leaving the magician with the other. The magician then explains it is critical that whatever he does, the spectator does precisely the same. He goes on to say that if this happens, the spectator will be able to do a magic trick. After shuffling their own packs, they exchange them. Each takes a card from the center of his new pack, remembers it, and cuts it back into the pack. They exchange decks again, leaving both the magician and the spectator with their original packs. They each look through their original pack and pull out the card matching the one they had selected in the other person's pack. The magician instructs the spectator, on the count of three, to turn over his card and call out its name loudly enough for all to hear, and says that he will do the same. This is done, and both cards are shown to be the same.

METHOD

STEP 1: You will need two packs of cards: a red one and a blue one. Have the spectator select one, leaving you with the other. Explain that this trick is called "You Do as I Do" and that if he does exactly what you do, he will be able to do the same magic trick.

★

STEP 2: Pause and scratch your forehead. Keep on doing this for a few seconds. If and when the spectator starts to copy you, congratulate him. If a few seconds go by and he does not start, just give him a weird look, as if to say, "Anytime you're ready." When he starts to copy you, say, "Don't worry, it was just a test." This is sure to bring a few laughs, *without embarrassing or insulting the spectator.* (This is a point that is often forgotten by some professional magicians, who apparently believe that to be funny you have to embarrass or insult a member of the audience.)

★

STEP 3: Slowly and deliberately, open up the card case and remove the deck. The spectator, 99 percent of the time, will duplicate your movements. If he does not, give him a gentle reminder. At this point, the spectator will have gotten the drift.

★

STEP 4: Shuffle the cards, and the spectator will do the same. Comment that the decks are being thoroughly shuffled. When you are done shuffling, as you square up the pack, glance at the bottom card. This will be your "key" card. Do this in such a fashion so that nobody realizes that you did *anything.* If they do, the trick will be ruined.

★

STEP 5: Explain to the spectator that you will now switch packs with him. Do so.

★

STEP 6: Slowly reach into the spectator's pack, now in your hands, and pull out a card. The spectator will do the same. Look at it, but do not let anyone else see it. If they do, the trick will have failed. (There is no need to remember this card, just don't forget your key card on the bottom of the pack that is now in the spectator's hands.) The spectator will do the same, and instruct him to remember his card. You may want to remind him from time to time not to forget.

★

STEP 7: Slowly and deliberately place your selection on top of your pack, and the spectator will do the same. Keep an eye on him to make sure he is doing everything correctly. *Do not forget your key card at the bottom of your original pack.* Now carefully and slowly give your pack a straight cut, and the spectator will do the same. This will put your key card on top of his selected card.

★

STEP 8: Exchange packs again, leaving you with your original pack and the spectator with his original pack. Instruct the spectator to go through his original pack, now in his hands, and to take out his card. Instruct the spectator not to let anyone see the card and to place it face down on the table.

★

STEP 9: As the spectator is doing this, you run through your pack looking for your key card. When you find it, take out the card directly on top of it (fig.1). This is the card that the spectator selected. Place this card face down on the table, side by side with the spectator's card. If you're presenting this trick before a large audience, have the spectator face the au-

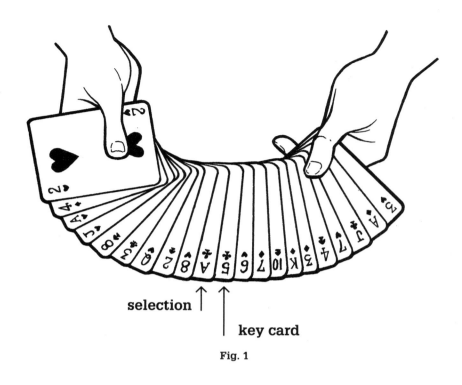

selection ↑ ↑

key card

Fig. 1

COMMENTS

★

A great value of this trick is that it plays equally well on stage as it does close up. If you have a special occasion where you want to enhance the mystery, use two brand new, sealed decks of cards, still in their wrappers. Have the spectator choose one of the decks, and both of you simultaneously unwrap the decks and break the seals.

dience and hold his card with its face against his chest. You do the same.

★

STEP 10: Keep in mind that up until now, no magic has happened. Therefore, you must really build up the revelation that the two cards are the same. Tell the spectator that on the count of three he should turn over his card so the audience can see it and simultaneously call out the name of it. You say you'll do the same.

★

STEP 11: Count—1 . . . 2 . . . 3! The ___ of ___ will be yelled in unison, which will be directly followed by wild applause.

NOTE
★

I became interested in magic at the age of five, when my father did a magic show at my birthday party. My interest never got serious, and actually faded, until the summer of 1992. A counselor at my summer camp, David Fattel, an excellent close-up magician, rekindled my interest. This was one of the first tricks I learned when I got back into magic. It was originated by mentalist/magician Al Baker.

Suzy Clattrel, a mentalist, performed an elaborate version of this trick on the *Tonight Show with Johnny Carson* in the 1970s. Carson, an experienced magician himself, was completely fooled.

Three-Way Prediction

EFFECT

The deck is shuffled. About twenty cards are scattered face down on the table. The magician names a card and invites the spectator to reach into the mess of cards and attempt to slide out the one he thinks is the named card. The magician peeks at it, congratulates the spectator on his good intuition, and leaves the card, still face down, on the table. This is repeated with a second card. Finally, a third card is named and this time the magician himself slides out a card. He congratulates both the spectator and himself for good intuition. The magician turns over the three cards, and they are the exact cards that had been named.

METHOD

STEP 1: Shuffle the cards. You must gain knowledge of the top card in the course of shuffling. Let me briefly describe one technique that can be used, using the overhand shuffle. Hold the deck in your left hand, at chest level, backs facing the audience. Your right shoulder faces the audience as well. Your left hand is comfortably positioned under the deck, thumb against the face of the deck, fingers along the bottom. The right hand rests on the back of it, holding the deck by its edges, with the index finger resting on the top long edge (fig. 1).

Fig. 1

Take the card on the face of the deck, remembering its name, into your left hand (fig. 2). Now drop about a third of the remaining cards into the left hand on top of the card already there (fig. 3). Drop about half of the cards remaining in the right hand into the left in the same fashion as before. Finally, drop all of the remaining cards from the right hand into the left. This will leave the card you noted on top of the deck. Now, you may wish to riffle shuffle the cards as described in step 3 of "Speller," found on page 54; being sure to let the top card fall last so it remains on top of the deck. Do not forget this card.

Fig. 2

Fig. 3

★

STEP 2: Scatter about twenty cards on the table. If you want to, you may even want to scatter the whole deck on the table. Remember, however, where the top card is on the table so that you will be able to pull it out without hesitation when needed.

★

STEP 3: Instruct the spectator that this will be an experiment involving intuition and that it may not work. (This is not true, but it will make the impact greater when the spectator sees that it does indeed work out.) Tell him that you have scattered about twenty cards on the table. Then say that you will name a card and that he is to slide the one out that he thinks is the named card.

★

STEP 4: Name the card that was the card originally on the top of the deck. The spectator should think that you just called out a card at random. He will now pull out any card, it does not matter which one (fig. 4). Be sure neither the spectator nor anyone else sees its face.

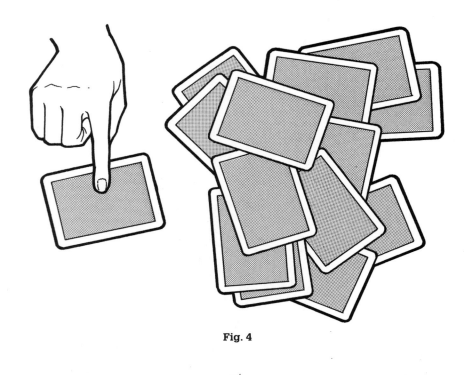

Fig. 4

★

STEP 5: Openly look at the card he pulled out. Do not let anyone else see it. If by chance, the spectator happens to pick the card you named, turn it over and end the trick. This does indeed occasionally happen. Otherwise, look at the spectator and congratulate him, saying that he has good intuition, as if he actually took the named card. Hold on to the card he pulled out.

★

STEP 6: Now you will name the card the spectator just pulled out that you had looked at, and have the spectator pull out a second card. Once again, if the spectator pulls out the original top card, turn over both cards and conclude the trick. Otherwise, as before, look at the second card, making sure nobody else sees it, and congratulate the spectator on his good intuition. Hold on to the second card along with the first.

★

STEP 7: Now you will name the second card the spectator pulled out. Once again, the spectator should think that this was a random choice. This time, you will pull out a card. Reach into the mess of cards and pull out the original top card. Now, in your hand you will have the three cards you named.

★

STEP 8: Look at the three cards and comment that it seems that the experiment has worked. As you say this, mix the cards just a little. This will make it impossible for anyone to realize they are out of order. Look the spectator in the eyes, pause, and slowly turn over the three cards, revealing a miracle.

C O M M E N T S
★

In this trick, if performed properly, the spectator will not know that the cards were picked out of sequence. Also, the spectator should not suspect the cards you are naming are anything other than random choices.

Another way of presenting this is to use two spectators. Have each of them select a card, and you take a third. The trick will come out exactly the same way. And if you are worried that the three cards will be forgotten, have the spectator(s) write down the names of the cards you call off. This will eliminate all possibility of forgetfulness.

NOTE
★

In many of the card tricks that follow, a spectator will be asked to
select a card. The most common
way to present the deck for a
selection is the Hand-to-Hand
Spread. While relatively easy to
do, it is often not done correctly.
When this happens, it looks
sloppy. Another, prettier way to
spread the deck is the Ribbon
Spread, but you often do not have
enough room on a clean table to
spread the deck. I will explain
both and leave it up to you to
judge when each is appropriate.

Hand-to-Hand and Ribbon Spreads

The Hand-to-Hand Spread

STEP 1: Hold the deck in a left-hand mechanic's grip, as described in "To Control a Card to the Bottom of the Deck," on page 56. Your left thumb begins to push over cards from the top of the deck (fig. 1).

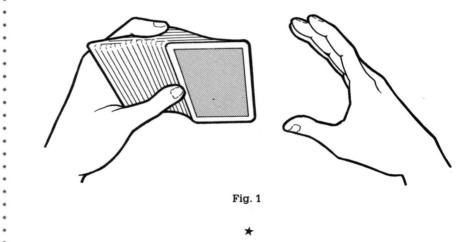

Fig. 1

★

STEP 2: Bring your right hand to the cards, fingers on bottom and thumb on top, and hold on to the cards already pushed over. Your left thumb continues to push cards toward your right hand until the deck has been spread into an approximate ten-inch arc (fig. 2). This is

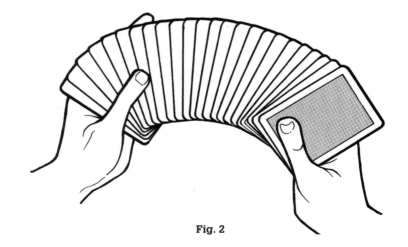

Fig. 2

the Hand-to-Hand Spread. To close it, simply move the right hand to the left, collecting the spread cards back on top of the deck in the left hand.

The Ribbon Spread

STEP 1: For this you must have a clear, clean surface. Hold the deck with your right hand as shown in fig. 3. (This is from the performer's view.) Bring the deck onto the table, continuing to hold it the same way, in your right hand, the tip of your index finger resting lightly on the table (again, fig. 3, from the performer's view).

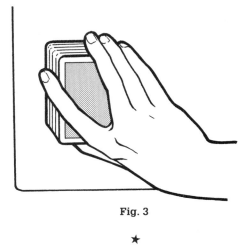

Fig. 3

★

STEP 2: While applying downward pressure, begin to move the hand and deck to the right, while only loosely applying pressure against the side of the deck with the index finger. What will happen is depicted in fig. 4. (This is from a performer's view). The deck will begin to spread evenly. It takes a knack, but with some practice, it will come easily. The deck should finally end up being spread evenly about eighteen inches.

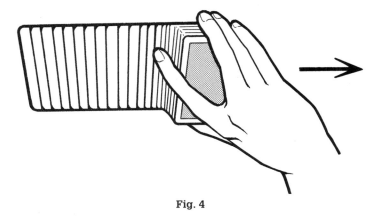

Fig. 4

Speller

The deck is shuffled. A card is selected by a spectator and replaced inside the deck. The deck is then shuffled again. The spectator is then asked to state his name. The magician deals one card to the table for each letter of the spectator's name. The last card dealt turns out to be the spectator's previously selected card.

METHOD

STEP 1: Have the deck shuffled by a spectator, or do it yourself. Have the spectator select a card.

★

STEP 2: Execute the "To Control a Card to the Bottom of the Deck," as described on page 56. At the end of that sleight, the deck will be on the table.

★

STEP 3: Riffle shuffle the cards. The riffle shuffle is commonly used in card games and by magicians. Each hand takes half the deck, and holds it, back side facing the palm, between the thumb on one short side and the middle, ring, and pinkie fingers on the other. The index fingers are curled and apply pressure on top of their respective halves. The hands rest next to each other on the table, with the thumbs facing each other. The thumbs pull up on the short sides of the deck (fig. 1).

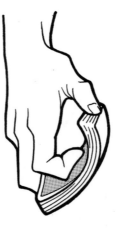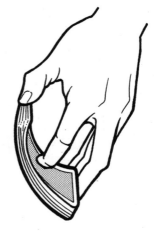

Fig. 1

Now, the thumbs release pressure, allowing the cards to fall and interlace as they do so (fig. 2). Take care not to expose the bottom card.

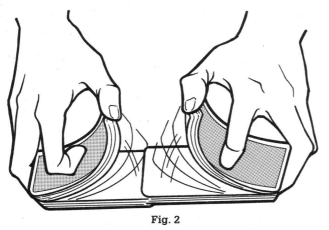

Fig. 2

Be sure to have the bottom card, which the spectator selected, fall first, so it remains on the bottom of the deck. Square up the deck and place it, face down, on the table.

If you cannot do this shuffle, any shuffle that will keep the bottom card in place will suffice. At the end, place the deck face down on the table.

★

STEP 4: Pick the deck up with your left hand, palm down, which will leave you in a glide grip, as described in the sleight "The Glide" on page 60.

★

STEP 5: Do the slide-back technique (see "The Glide"). You are now ready to perform the pull-out, or the heart of "The Glide."

★

STEP 6: Ask the spectator to state his name. After that, ask him to spell it slowly.

★

STEP 7: For each letter, draw out the second card from the bottom, as described in the pull-out, and place each one face down on the table.

★

STEP 8: On the last letter, really draw out the bottom card. Do not place it on the table; leave it in your hand.

★

STEP 9: Ask the spectator to name his card, which he does. *Pause*—this is important—and slowly reveal the card in your hand to be the selected card. You have just performed a miracle.

C O M M E N T S

★

This trick is a good example of how getting a spectator involved in the trick can make it more powerful. There can be many variations of this trick. For instance, you can ask the spectator to pick a number, and you would supposedly count out that number of cards from the bottom of the deck, producing the selected card at the last position. This trick works equally well for adults and children.

To Control a Card to the Bottom of the Deck

Controlling a selected card to the bottom of the deck is an important tool of card conjuring. To begin, have a spectator select a card. I usually use either the hand-to-hand spread or the ribbon spread. When the spectator has a card, return the deck to mechanic's grip, as described below.

Mechanic's Grip

Mechanic's grip is a way of holding cards that you will see time and again in this book. It is the grip best suited for most sleights and also a grip that will feel comfortable in your hands. Hold the deck face down, in the palm-up left hand, short sides facing you and the audience. The middle, ring, and pinkie fingers are on the right long side of the deck, with the thumb curled over the left long side, but relaxed. The index finger is on the short side of the deck, which faces the audience. The deck should be very close to the palm, as you might hold it when dealing in a game of cards (fig. 1).

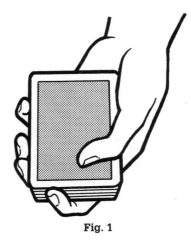

Fig. 1

To Obtain a Pinkie Break

STEP 1: With the deck in left-hand mechanic's grip, the right hand comes over the deck, palm down.

★

STEP 2: Now, move your left thumb to the left edge of the deck. The right hand now takes approximately half the cards from the top of the deck, with the right fingers at the front short side of the deck and the thumb at the opposing side.

★

STEP 3: The left hand now extends toward the spectator, inviting him to replace the selected card on top of the half you extend toward him *and reminding him not to forget it.* As this is happening, you are simultaneously preparing yourself to control his card, as explained in the steps that follow.

★

STEP 4: As you move your hand toward him, your left pinkie presses against the left side of the cards right where it is, leaving a little bit of flesh extending a few millimeters over the top card (fig. 2). When he puts the card on top of this half, your pinkie will create a break between his card and the rest of that half (fig. 3).

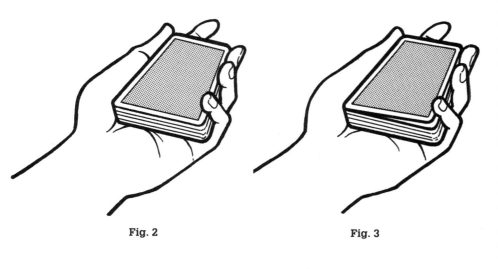

Fig. 2   Fig. 3

★

STEP 5: The right hand replaces the balance of the cards on top of the cards already in the left hand, making sure to keep your left pinkie in place so as not to release the break; the spectator's card is above your pinkie.

★

STEP 6: Carefully square up the deck, keeping the break. You have now successfully obtained a pinkie break (fig. 4). Make sure you do not "leak," or have a seam in the front of the deck where the break is. Once you have gained a break, your right hand is free to gesture, a form of misdirection.

Fig. 4

The Three-Way Cut

You've learned the hard part: you have a pinkie break below the selected card. Now you are ready to bring the selected card to the bottom.

★

STEP 1: Move your right hand over the deck and lift from the deck all of the cards above your break, approximately half the deck, and place it onto the table (fig. 5).

Fig. 5

★

STEP 2: Bring your right hand over the cards remaining in your left hand. Take half of these cards, in the same manner as before, and place them on top of the cards already on the table.

★

STEP 3: Finally, your right hand comes over the left hand a third time, takes the remaining cards, and places them on top of the ones already on the table. In the eyes of the audience, you've just completed a three-way cut of the deck. The whole deck should now be reassembled on the table, with the selected card at the bottom of the deck. Pretty cool, eh?

Practice all of this in front of a mirror until you can do it smoothly, without hesitating. Using this combination of sleights, you can perform many card miracles.

The Glide

The glide is one of the oldest, simplest card sleights. It goes back to the early magic text *Modern Magic,* by Professor Hoffman. (That was his stage name. His real name was Angelo Lewis.) When used in conjunction with the control of a selected card to the bottom of the deck, it has a wide variety of applications. If these instructions are followed carefully, and you practice in front of a mirror, you will have learned to perform a great sleight.

The Glide Grip

The glide grip is the way you hold the deck of cards for the glide. Start out with the deck face up in your left hand, palm up, with the short sides facing you and the audience. All of the fingers of the left hand curl around the right side of the deck, with the thumb gently curled over the left. As in mechanic's grip, the deck is held close to the palm, as if you were dealing cards. To prepare properly for the glide, the deck should protrude forward from the front of your hand so that your pinkie rests on the inner right corner of the deck. Finally, to get into glide grip, simply turn your left hand, deck and all, palm down. The deck's long sides are now facing you and the audience. You are now in glide grip (fig. 1). (This sequence should not be employed in performance. It is simply to guide you into the glide grip. In performance, it is a simple matter to pick the deck off the table in glide grip.)

Fig. 1

The Slide-Back Technique

The slide-back technique is basically a preparation for the pull-out. At this point, the deck should be in left-hand glide grip. The move is not complicated. Basically, under the cover of the deck, the middle, ring, and pinkie fingers apply slight pressure to the bottom of the deck and pull back, dragging the bottom card along with them (fig. 2). The ring and pinkie fingers will mask the protruding bottom card. You are now set for the final pull-out.

Fig. 2

The Pull-Out

At this point, the deck should be as shown in Figure 2. Your right hand comes under what is now the right short side of the deck. The middle finger contacts the card above the card that has been drawn back. The finger slides it out, as if it were the bottom card. As soon as possible, contact the top of this card with your thumb (fig. 3). Draw the card out and place it on the table. You may repeat this as many times as you like, as the original bottom card will always stay on the bottom. The preceding trick, "Speller," uses the glide in a powerful way.

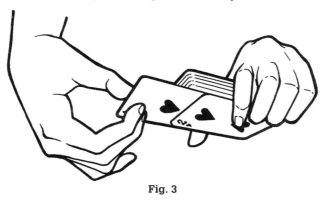

Fig. 3

NOTE
★

This trick was originated by Dai Vernon, generally considered to be the greatest contributor to the art of close-up magic. The original version of "Triumph" appeared in a pamphlet, *Stars of Magic, Series 2, No. 2*, published by Louis Tannen, Inc., and was subsequently included in an anthology entitled, *Stars of Magic.* This "sleightly" (pardon the pun) less difficult version that follows was created by magician Sid Lorraine and appeared in a magazine called *Jinx*, for many years an important magic publication.

In Vernon's memoirs, *The Man Who Fooled Houdini*, he describes his "fantasy Triumph." His fantasy was to have a card selected and returned to the deck and the deck shuffled. He and the spectator would then go up in a helicopter and hover about fifty feet above an ocean. The deck would be thrown out of the helicopter and the cards would scatter and settle on the ocean below. All of the cards would be face down, except one, the selected card!

Triumph

EFFECT

The deck of cards is shuffled, and the spectator selects a card. He looks at it and replaces it in the deck. The performer then mixes the cards in a very odd manner, leaving some face up, some face down, all different combinations, a real mess. He then snaps his fingers and spreads the deck face up on the table. All the cards are shown to be facing the same way, except for one in the center, which turns out to be the selected card.

METHOD

STEP 1: Have the cards shuffled, either by you or the spectator. Then spread the deck from hand to hand, or ribbon spread it on the table. Have the spectator select a card. Remind the spectator not to let you see the card. While he is looking at the card, gather the deck into a pack with your right hand and casually drop your hand, holding the deck, to your side. While it is there, bend the pack so that it has a somewhat concave shape (fig. 1). Do this inconspicuously.

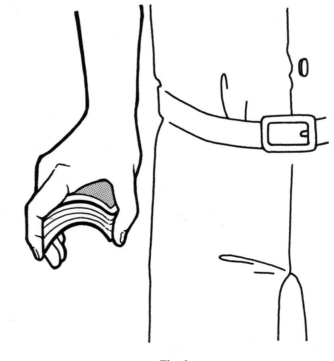

Fig. 1

STEP 2: Execute "To Control a Card to the Bottom of the Deck," page 56.

★

STEP 3: You are now going to mix the cards using something known as the "slop" shuffle. Hold the deck face down, in left-hand mechanic's grip, described in "To Control a Card to the Bottom of the Deck." With your thumb, push off about seven cards or so. The number does not have to be exact. Bring your right hand over, palm up, and take these cards with all four of your right-hand fingers under them and the thumb on top.

Now rotate your right hand, turning the cards face up and your hand palm down (figs. 2 and 3). Thumb off another group of cards from the left hand. Take these under the ones you already have, holding them

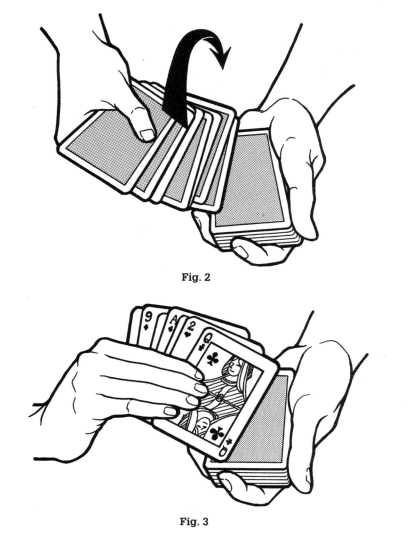

Fig. 2

Fig. 3

there with your right thumb (fig. 4). Rotate the right hand back over so that it is palm-up. Thumb off another group of cards from the left hand and take them under the cards you already have in your right hand. Repeat this pattern until only the bottom or selected card remains in your left hand, face down.

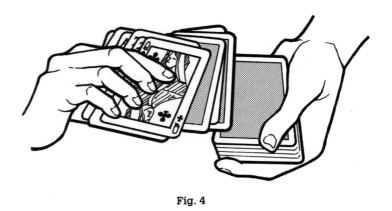

Fig. 4

★

STEP 4: The cards in your right hand are now arranged so that half are facing one way and half the other. The audience should think that every seven cards or so, the orientation changes. Rotate your right hand so that it is palm up. Now, the top card of the right-hand pack should be face up and the selected card in your left hand, face down. Without hesitation, place this last card face down, on top of the deck. (The spectator should have no knowledge that this is his card, nor should he realize you treated it any differently than the others.) After this is done, I offer a small joke, asking, "Do you know what this shuffle is called?" When they say "no," I say, "A mess." Ha, ha, ha.

★

STEP 5: Your situation is this: The top, face-down card is the selected card. From then on, about half the deck is face up, the bottom half face down. The spectator should think the cards are randomly mixed, face up and face down. Explain that the cards are quite mixed. Hold the deck in left-hand mechanic's grip. Bring the right hand over the deck, palm down. Lift up about the top quarter of the deck, showing a face-up card on top of the packet in your left hand. Say, "Some cards are face up." Replace the portion in your right hand back onto the cards in your left hand. Then lift up about three-quarters of the deck, revealing a face-down card. Say, "Some cards are face down." Replace the right-hand packet back on the left-hand packet.

★

STEP 6: Finally, lift up the packet of cards above the separation in the center of the deck, at the point where the two halves meet. This is easy because of the bend you gave the deck at the beginning. Show the bottom of the packet you lift up by rotating your right hand palm up; hold that position. The spectator will see the back of a card. He'll also see the back of a card atop the packet in your left hand. You can now say, "Some cards are even back to back." Place the packet in your right hand, atop the packet in your left hand, keeping your right hand palm up (fig. 5). This will put the selected card at the center of the deck, the only one reversed.

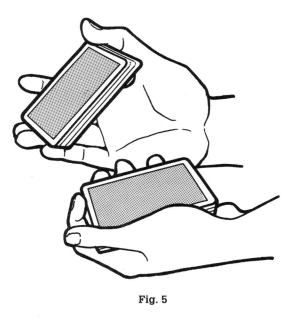

Fig. 5

★

STEP 7: Snap your fingers, and say some magic words. Pause a moment. Slowly spread the deck on the table, revealing that all of the cards have righted themselves, except for the selected card.

Of all of the card tricks in this section, this is probably the one I perform the most.

Card-in-Envelope Prediction

EFFECT

A sealed envelope is removed from the magician's pocket. Inside the envelope, he says, there is a card. The deck is shuffled and a card selected. The envelope is opened, and inside is found a card that is exactly the same as the one the spectator just selected.

PREPARATION

You'll need a small tan envelope with both a glue seal and a metal clasp. Also, get an extra playing card with a back design or color other than that of the deck you'll use for this effect. Place the card inside the envelope, seal it, and place it inside your pocket. Do not forget the name of the card. Now, from the deck, put the card that matches the one in the envelope on to the face of the deck, and place the deck in its box. You are all set to go.

METHOD

STEP 1: Take the sealed envelope from your pocket and place it on the table. Say that you have placed a card, a prediction, inside it.

★

STEP 2: Remove the deck from its case. Invite a spectator to select a card. Force the bottom card, via the "Hindu-Shuffle Force," as described on page 67. Place the portion of the deck with the "freely selected" card on its face, face up on the table. Emphasize that the spectator could have selected any card in the deck. Of course, this is not true. From the spectator's point of view, however, he had full freedom of choice.

★

STEP 3: Hand the envelope to the spectator and have him open it. Inside he will find a duplicate of the selected card.

Hindu-Shuffle Force

M E T H O D

STEP 1: Have the card you want to force on the bottom or face of the deck. You will now begin what is known as the Hindu shuffle.

★

STEP 2: Hold the deck with the tips of the fingers of your right hand. Your middle and ring fingers and thumb barely extend past the bottom of the deck. The index finger rests on the back of the deck. The pinkie plays no role in the grip and does not touch the deck (fig. 1).

Fig. 1

★

STEP 3: Your left hand now grips the deck, palm up, index finger curled around the front, short side of the deck, thumb along the left side, and the remaining fingers on the right, long side of the deck. The left fingers and thumb now apply pressure to the group of cards at the top of the deck. Holding on to them, your right hand pulls back, leaving the group of cards from the top of the deck in your left hand (fig. 2). Let the cards in your left hand fall to your palm (fig. 3). They will fall in a position close to mechanic's grip. You will repeat the move rapidly, again and again, each time taking a small packet and letting it fall on to the cards resting on your left palm (fig. 4).

N O T E

★

The Hindu shuffle is called such because that is how the natives of India were seen to shuffle cards by European travelers during the time India was a British colony.

Forcing a card means to make sure, secretly, that the spectator selects the card you want him to. This force is easy to do, very deceiving if done in a flowing, smooth motion, and simply cannot miss.

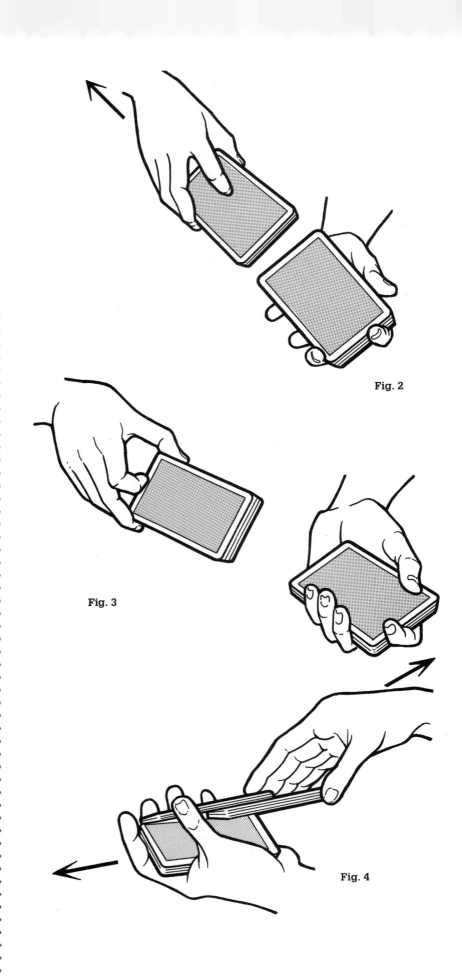

Fig. 2

Fig. 3

Fig. 4

★

STEP 4: As you start the Hindu shuffle, say to the spectator, "I want you to say, 'stop,' anywhere."

★

STEP 5: When the spectator does say "stop," lift the cards in your right hand, showing the spectator the face of the card at the bottom of the packet (fig. 5). He will believe that he picked a random card, when really he picked the card that was the original bottom card, the force card.

If this sleight is done at a fairly rapid pace, and smoothly, the spectator will be wholly unaware that he didn't have a free choice of cards.

Fig. 5

Are You Sure?

EFFECT

The deck is shuffled. A card is selected by the spectator. It is returned to the deck. The deck is shuffled and cut. The magician claims the selected card is on the top of the deck. The top card is turned over but is not the selected card. It is put on the table. The magician asks for the name of the card and spreads the deck. It is shown that the selected card is not in the deck. The original top card, the one on the table, is turned over and is shown to have changed into the selected card.

METHOD

STEP 1: Have the deck shuffled. Then, have a card selected.

★

STEP 2: Execute the "To Control a Card to the Top of the Deck," as described on page 72.

★

STEP 3: Riffle shuffle the deck. (See step 3 of "Speller," page 54.) Be sure, in this case, to let the top few cards fall last so that the selected card stays on top.

★

STEP 4: Claim that the top card is the selected card. Execute the "Double Lift," as described on page 74. This will show that the apparent "top card" is not the selected card.

★

STEP 5: Immediately take the real top card, which is the selected card, and place it face down on the table. The spectator should not know that this is his card. As soon as you have placed the card down, you may want to give the deck a cut to lose the card you just displayed.

★

STEP 6: Ask the spectator to name his card. When he does, spread the deck face up on the table. His card, of course, is not to be seen.

STEP 7: Give the spectator a moment to realize that his card is not in the deck. With a slight note of impatience in your voice, say, "I give up. Let's just find your card and end the trick." Then ask, "What was the name of your card again?" He will repeat the name of the card.

★

STEP 8: Slowly turn over the card that is face down on the table and reveal the miracle. While your audience reacts with astonishment, gather up the cards and take a bow.

Of all of the complicated, and not so complicated, sleights that I know and use, this is by far the one I use the most. Once a card is on the top of the deck, you can do anything with it.

Television Magic

*I*n addition to numerous magic specials, there were several regular TV shows that brought magic into the homes of millions of Americans, stimulating the growing interest in magic as entertainment. Bob McAllister, a magician and teacher of magic, was host of two popular children's shows, *Wonderama,* and later, *Kids Are People, Too,* which together ran for more than two decades into the 1980s on national television. In almost every show, McAllister would either perform magic, teach a trick, or have a magician as a guest. Ventriloquist and magician Shari Lewis, in her long-running daily show, *Baby Lambchop,* taught a trick on almost every episode. Mark Wilson, author of the *Mark Wilson Course in Magic,* a popular beginner's magic book, was host of the *Magic Land of Alacazam.* This thirty-minute show, which started out as a cartoon with a five-minute magic segment, ended up being almost all magic. The late actor Bill Bixby, of *Incredible Hulk* fame, was star of a weekly television show called *The Magician,* in which he played a magician who solved crimes. These shows and others inspired many of today's top magicians and helped popularize magic.

To Control a Card to the Top of the Deck

Pinkie Break Above

STEP 1: Have a card selected.

★

STEP 2: Hold the deck in left-hand mechanic's grip, as described in "To Control a Card to the Bottom of the Deck," page 56. Bring the right hand, palm down, over the deck, with your thumb against the back, short side of the deck. Lift about half the cards off the deck.

★

STEP 3: Now, here's where it begins to differ from the control to the bottom. Extend the half in your left hand to the spectator. Have the selected card replaced normally on top of the left half. Do not obtain a pinkie break below the card.

★

STEP 4: After it is replaced, apply pressure with the left-hand pinkie against the left-hand side of the deck, right where it is. This is basically the same action as in step 4 of "To Control a Card to the Bottom of the Deck" (fig. 1).

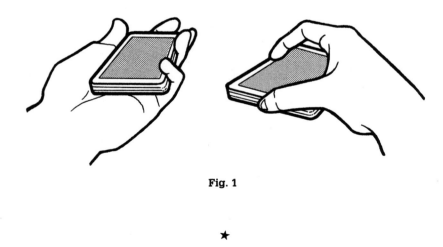

Fig. 1

★

STEP 5: Replace the half that is in the right hand, on top of the half in the left hand. Retain the break.

Three-Way Cut to Top

STEP 1: At this point, the deck should be in left-hand mechanic's grip, with a pinkie break on top of the selected card. Bring your right hand over the deck, palm down. With your right thumb against the back short side, lift off half of the cards above your break. Place these on the table (fig. 2).

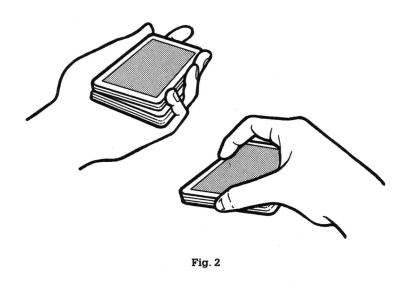

Fig. 2

★

STEP 2: In the same fashion, your right hand will now take all of the remaining cards above the break and place them on top of the ones already on the table.

★

STEP 3: Finally, your right hand will come over the left hand one last time. Take all of the remaining cards and place them on top of the cards already on the table. This will have brought the selected card to the top of the deck, which rests on the table.

Double Lift

STEP 1: Hold the deck in left-hand mechanic's grip, as described in "To Control a Card to the Bottom of the Deck," page 56. Bring the right hand over the deck, palm down, and press the right thumb against the back, short side of the deck. The index finger curls over and rests on the top of the deck. The other three fingers rest on the front, short side of the deck. Now, the tip of your right thumb applies slight pressure to the lower portion of the back, short side of the deck. The deck will bevel, as shown in fig. 1.

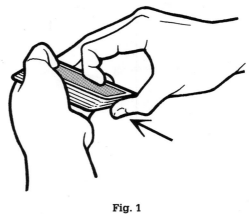

Fig. 1

★

STEP 2: Now with your right thumb, as gently as possible, lift up two cards, as shown in fig. 2.

Fig. 2

STEP 3: The front edge of the deck, the side the audience sees, should look perfectly normal, as should the top of the deck. However, your view of the back edge of the deck will show two cards lifted by your right thumb. The two cards will be about a millimeter or two apart, as depicted in fig. 2. Slightly loosen the thumb's pressure on the edge of the top card, allowing it to fall directly on to the second card.

★

STEP 4: Now the two top cards are about an eighth of an inch above the rest of the deck, one directly on top of the other. You now have a thumb break under the double. Continue to apply pressure as you slide your thumb and fingers to the left (fig. 3). This will leave you in a position as shown in fig. 4.

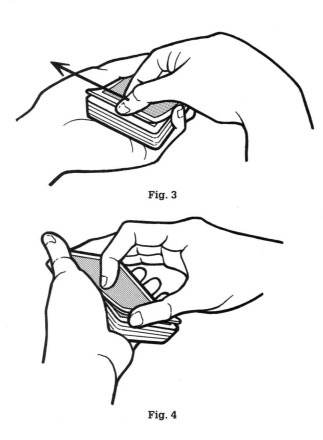

Fig. 3

Fig. 4

★

STEP 5: Curl your left hand's lower three fingers slightly over the right-hand, long side of the deck. The right hand, using the thumb on one side and the middle finger on the other, lifts the double up and to the right (fig. 5), hinging on the left-hand fingers. (In fig. 5 and other illustrations that show two cards held as one, an extra edge is used to indicate the hidden card. This is simply for clarity and should not show in performance.) This movement is much like opening the back cover of a book.

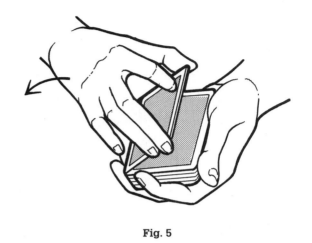

Fig. 5

★

STEP 6: When the double is at a 90° angle with the deck, the back of the double will hit the pads of the top joints of the lower three left-hand fingers. At this point, move your right hand's index finger from the back side of the double to the face side.

★

STEP 7: Continue moving the double to the right, and the bottom long edge will begin to slide to the left along the back of the top card of the deck. The left fingers are now being used as a pivot point (fig. 6).

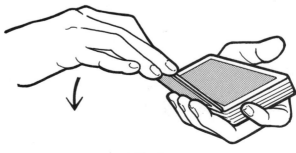

Fig. 6

Stop moving the double to the right when you reach about a 160° angle (fig. 7).

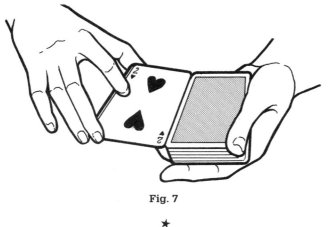

Fig. 7

★

STEP 8: At this point the double is held between the right-hand middle finger and thumb, with the index finger resting on the double's face side. Slowly begin to move the double to the left. As you do this, your left-hand pinkie applies pressure against the right, long side of the deck, and a little bit of flesh will extend over the top card (fig. 8).

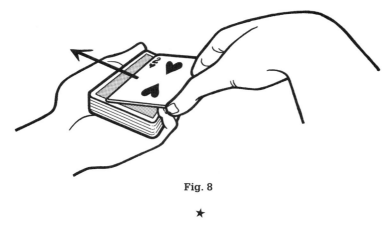

Fig. 8

★

STEP 9: Continue moving the double to the left until it hits the left thumb base (fig. 9).

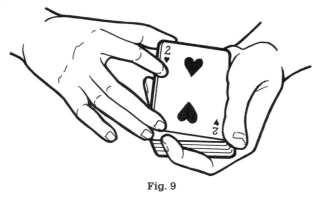

Fig. 9

This is a *very* important sleight. Do not let the long description discourage you from learning it. As a matter of fact, the entire sleight takes only about five seconds or less, not exactly in proportion with the description.

Keep in mind that the audience should have no knowledge that you are dealing with more than one card.

Also, this is one of the harder card sleights in the book. If you do wish to learn it, give it a lot of practice before you perform it. It deserves it. Concentrate on doing steps 2 and 3 smoothly, as they are extremely difficult. Also, since the audience should believe that you are only dealing with one card, if you have occasion to turn over the top card normally, do it exactly the same way you do in the double lift. This way, the audience will see consistency in the way you handle cards. This is a good rule for any sleight you do in magic.

★

STEP 10: Now move the card downward, until you hit the flesh of the left-hand pinkie. At this point, let go with the right hand, leaving a pinkie break under the face-up double. This is so you are able to turn the card(s) back over (fig. 10).

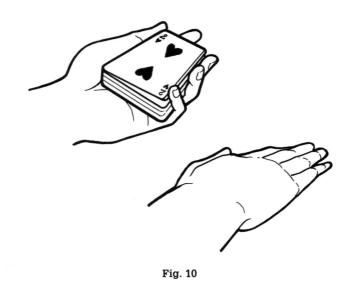

Fig. 10

★

STEP 11: To turn the double back over, bring your right hand back over the deck, palm down. Apply pressure against the back, short side of the deck with your thumb, and you will be in the same position you were at the end of step 3.

★

STEP 12: You will now basically repeat steps 4–10 to turn the card back over. The only difference is that here, you will relieve pressure of the left pinkie against the side of the deck. This way, when the double hits the thumb base and you move it down, the pinkie will be out of the way and you will not have a pinkie break.

Card to Wallet

EFFECT

The deck is shuffled. The spectator selects a card and signs it with a marker (optional). The card is returned to the deck, which is then cut and shuffled. The performer, with a clearly empty hand, takes out his wallet. He opens it. Inside is a card, face down. It is turned over and shown to be the same card that the spectator selected, with his signature on it.

PREPARATION

If you carry a deck of cards, remove one of the cards. If not, purchase a red Bicycle deck, as this is by far the most common, and remove one of its cards. In any case, take this card and place it in your wallet. I usually place the card in an inner compartment, preferably one with a zipper. When the card is revealed, this makes it seem even more impossible. Or, if you want to take a little extra time but enhance the mystery, place the card within a sealed envelope and place the envelope in your wallet.

The card should be placed in such a way that when you take it out, it's face down. Keep your wallet in a pocket that is accessible to your right hand.

METHOD

STEP 1: Take out your deck of cards or borrow one. If the one you borrow is not a red Bicycle deck, perform another trick. If it is, carry on. Have the deck shuffled.

★

STEP 2: Have a spectator select and memorize a card. If you wish, and have access to a "Sharpie" marker (most other markers or pens cannot write on playing cards), have the spectator sign the selected card. Although this may ruin the card, I always do it this way, because it greatly enhances the trick. (If it is not your deck *do not* have the card signed.)

★

STEP 3: Execute the "To Control a Card to the Top of the Deck," as described on page 72.

NOTE

★

There are many ways of doing this classic trick. This is by far the simplest and easiest method. Don't be put off by the length of the instruction. This does not mean that it is any more difficult than other tricks in this book. It just means that I felt it was important that you know the details and nuances that make this a marvelous card trick. Take the time to learn it. It is without question worth the effort.

Ace Greenberg

Alan C. "Ace" Greenberg, chairman of Bear Stearns & Co., Inc., stock brokerage and investment banking firm, is one of Wall Street's best-known executives. Greenberg has been performing magic since childhood when he saw a show performed by Harry Blackstone, Sr., in Oklahoma City, where he grew up. "It just knocked my socks off," Greenberg recalls.

Greenberg performs for different charities and will often perform for guests at his house. "Magic is a great hobby," he says. "I don't care where I am, if I have a few minutes to spare, I can just take out a deck of cards and entertain myself. You don't need golf clubs or a tennis racket, just a little deck of cards or maybe some coins." He frequently performs magic at business gatherings and meetings and at the annual Christmas party for the children of Bear Stearns employees. However, he stresses that it is important not to overdo it. "You can't just walk up to somebody and say, 'Take a card.'" Greenberg adds, "My sister Di-Anne used to say that for my birthday present she'd watch five card tricks."

STEP 4: Riffle shuffle the cards, as described in step 3 of "Speller," page 54. However, as in "Are You Sure?," be sure to let the top few cards fall last so the selected card stays on top.

STEP 5: Say that the selected card has vanished from the deck and traveled into your wallet.

STEP 6: With an open right hand, reach into the pocket that contains the wallet. The hand will be seen to be empty, but do not mention it. The deck should be face down in the left-hand mechanic's grip, as described in "To Control a Card to the Bottom of the Deck," on page 56. As you reach into your pocket, your left hand should fall to your side.

STEP 7: Pull out the wallet. As you do this, your left hand performs a secret and inconspicuous action. It simply pushes over the top card slightly and applies pressure with the left pinkie against the side of the deck, under the card (fig. 1). When you pull back the card to its original position, you will note that you have obtained a pinkie break under the selected card (fig. 2). The spectator should have no knowledge that this is going on.

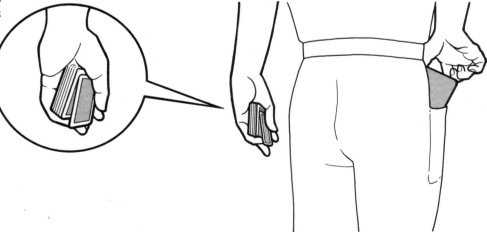

Fig. 1

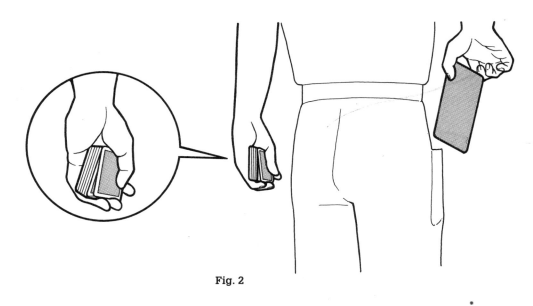

Fig. 2

★

STEP 8: Open up the wallet with both hands, using the fingers available to you: all of your right hand and the thumb and index finger of your left. Keep a firm grip on the deck, and do not lose your break.

If you use a zippered pocket, open it. Slowly slide out the face-down card and place it on top of the deck.

★

STEP 9: You will now have a pinkie break under the top two cards. To re-cap what the spectator sees: (1) The deck was shuffled. (2) A card was freely selected and signed. (3) The card was replaced in the deck and the deck shuffled again. (4) With an empty hand, you removed from your wallet a face-down card. (5) That card is now on top of the deck.

You will now bring your right hand, palm down, over the deck. Apply light pressure with your right thumb to the back, short side of the deck.

★

STEP 10: You will now execute steps 4–10 of the "Double Lift," described on page 74. Except, as you turn over the double, do not apply pressure with your left pinkie, as there is no need for a break. You will not need to turn back over the double. The card you have just revealed is the selected card.

★

STEP 11: Your situation is this: the deck is in left-hand mechanic's grip. The selected card is face up on top of the deck, with one other face-up card under it. Rotate your left hand over, turning your hand palm down and the deck face up. Turn your right hand palm up.

★

STEP 12: Under the deck, your left thumb pushes the top, selected card a half inch or so past the long edge of the deck (fig. 3). Your palm-up right hand takes the card, turns it face up, and gives it to the spectator who signed it. (If it is someone else's deck, and the card is not signed, *do not give it away.*) You only have one last thing to do: get rid of that face-up card on top of the deck.

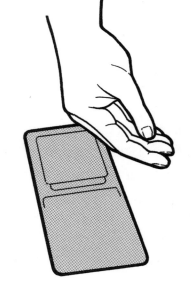

Fig. 3

★

STEP 13: If you are planning to do another trick, wait for a moment and enjoy the murmurs of amazement, the laughter, or applause you are bound to receive from your audience. After it subsides, just as you start introducing the next trick, let the top few cards of the deck fall to the table. Some will turn face up, others face down. Straighten the cards up, place them back on the deck, and continue. Act as if it was accidental. The audience should never know that you had to "clean up." I suggest you use this as your closing trick. It is definitely strong enough to serve as such. In this case, simply cut the cards face up, burying the reversed card somewhere in the middle of the deck. Immediately place the deck in its case.

Two-Card Transposition

EFFECT

A card case lies on the table. A spot card, such as the Nine of Clubs, is placed inside the empty card case. A court card, such as the King of Diamonds, is held in the magician's hand. The King is waved over the card case, and suddenly it is turned over, revealing that it has changed into the Nine of Clubs. When the case is opened, the card within is the King of Diamonds.

PREPARATION

For this effect, you will need to procure a duplicate of any court card in the deck, that is, two cards of the same suit and value, with the back of the duplicate matching the back of the original and of the entire deck. For now, we will assume the duplicates you have are two Kings of Diamonds. To set the deck, place one of the Kings on top of the deck. On top of that place any spot card (for now we will assume the Nine of Clubs), and on top of that place the remaining King. So, from the top down, you have King, Nine, King, rest of deck. You're all set.

METHOD

STEP 1: Take the deck and give it one riffle shuffle, as in step 3 of "Speller," described on page 54. Be sure to have the original top batch of cards fall last so that they stay on top.

★

STEP 2: Execute the "Double Lift," described on page 74, showing the Nine of Clubs. Once the card is turned face down, place the real top card, a King, inside the card case and close the case.

★

STEP 3: Execute another "Double Lift," this time showing one of the Kings. Once it has been turned back over, take the real top card, the Nine of Clubs, onto the table. Now, cut the deck to bury the duplicate King that is now on top of the deck. Put the deck aside.

N O T E
★
This trick is easy to execute and very easy to follow. The result, therefore, is all the more astonishing to the spectator. John Scarne, the famous card magician and casino gambling consultant, did this trick using a mug of beer rather than a card case, placing one card atop the mug and one under it. It was a performance that was widely used in a TV commercial for a major beer company.

★

STEP 4: Now pick up the tabled card, supposedly the King but really the Nine, and wave it over the case. Whenever you are ready, show that the card in your hand has changed to a Nine and have the case opened to reveal that the card within is a King.

Sandwich, Please

Two aces are removed from the deck and put on the table. The deck is shuffled. A card is selected by the spectator. It is placed back in the deck, which is then shuffled and cut. The two aces are picked up and shown front and back. The performer begins to shake the aces, and, slowly, a card begins to materialize, face down, between them. It is taken out, turned over, and shown to be the selected card.

METHOD

STEP 1: Go through the deck and remove two cards of the same value and color; I usually use the two red aces. Show them to the audience and place them, face down, on the table, explaining that they are very magical cards.

★

STEP 2: Shuffle the deck. Have a spectator select a card.

★

STEP 3: Execute the "To Control a Card to the Top of the Deck," as described on page 72.

★

STEP 4: Execute the riffle shuffle, as described in step 3 of "Speller," page 54. Be sure to let the top cards fall last, keeping the selected card on top of the deck.

★

STEP 5: Pick up the aces, and execute the "Classic Sandwich Technique," as described on page 88. This will leave the selected card, face down, hidden under the top ace. Both aces are exposed, side by side.

★

STEP 6: At this point, the deck is in your left hand, face down. Place it, with your left hand, still face down, on the table. Your right hand now places the spread two (but really three) cards, which are now held between the right middle finger and thumb, into the palm-up left hand (fig. 1). They are held there by the thumb firmly pressed against the face of the topmost ace (fig. 2).

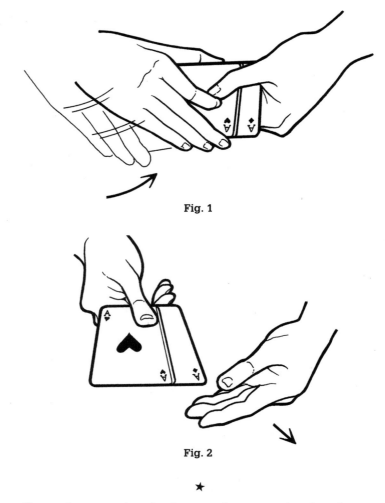

Fig. 1

Fig. 2

★

STEP 7: Grasp the spread at the bottom, between the thumb, on top, and the fingers of your right hand (fig. 3).

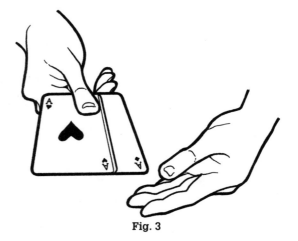

Fig. 3

STEP 8: Move your right hand, cards and all, away from the left hand. Slowly begin to shake the cards. The face-down card should still not be exposed.

★

STEP 9: Shake faster. When you're shaking the cards really fast, your right thumb applies pressure to the top card and moves to the right, slowly exposing the face-down card in the center (fig. 4). It will look as if it has just materialized there.

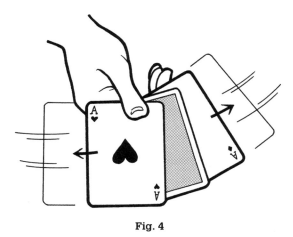

Fig. 4

★

STEP 10: At this point, stop shaking the cards. Your left hand removes the face-down card in the center and turns it face up on the table. It will be the spectator's selected card.

N O T E

★

This sleight, as far as I have been able to ascertain, was developed by the late Ed Marlo, specialist in card magic and one of the most innovative contributors to the art.

Classic Sandwich Technique

M E T H O D

STEP 1: You have on the table two mates, cards of the same value and color. The card you want to sandwich is on top of the deck, which is face down, in left-hand mechanic's grip, as described in "To Control a Card to the Bottom of the Deck," on page 56. Your left hand drops to your side, while your right hand gestures toward the cards on the table and you comment that they are "magical cards."

★

STEP 2: While this is happening, your left hand does the following: Slightly push the top card a few millimeters to the right, using your thumb. Your left pinkie now applies pressure against the right side of the deck, leaving a little bit of flesh extending over the right side of the deck and below the top card (fig. 1).

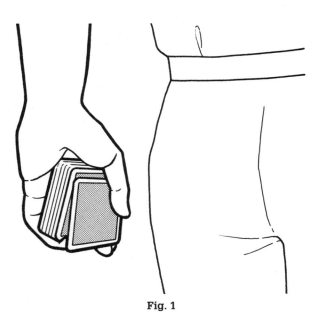

Fig. 1

★

STEP 3: With your left thumb, pull the card back over to the left. This will leave you with a pinkie break under the top card.

★

STEP 4: Bring your left hand, with the deck, back to a comfortable position in front of you. With your right hand, pick up the two aces, show both sides, and place them, squared, face up, on top of the deck. You will now have a pinkie break under the top three cards.

★

STEP 5: Now, your left thumb comes down and applies pressure to the top of the deck. Make sure to retain your break.

★

STEP 6: Your right hand comes over the deck, palm down, with your thumb on the back, short side, your middle and ring fingers on the front, short side. Your index finger curls over on the top of the deck.

★

STEP 7: The right thumb will now apply light pressure to the top three cards at the back, short side of the deck, giving you a right thumb break beneath the top three cards. Immediately, move your right hand, holding onto the edges of the three cards, to the right, still applying pressure to the top card with your left thumb. Make sure also to keep that left pinkie pressed up against the side of the deck because you will need it in a minute (fig. 2).

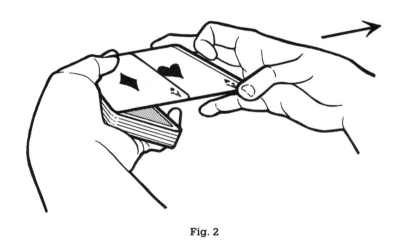

Fig. 2

★

STEP 8: What will happen, as shown in fig. 2, is that the top card will stay where it is, and the second and third cards, as one, will move to the right. Continue moving these two cards, as one, to the right, until they have cleared the top card. You will now have a break under the top ace.

The entire procedure takes less
than five seconds. You should be
able to do it very smoothly with
some practice.

★

STEP 9: Begin to move the two cards, as one, back to the left and over the top, face-up card under which you have a break. Stop when the double is about a quarter to a half inch from the left edge of the deck (fig. 3). Your right thumb and middle finger, which were holding the double, are now automatically gripping the bottom ace as well, which is elevated above the rest of the deck because of the pinkie break.

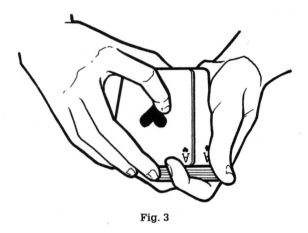

Fig. 3

★

STEP 10: Now, lift up everything above the break: the bottom ace and the top ace, which has one card directly beneath it (fig. 4).

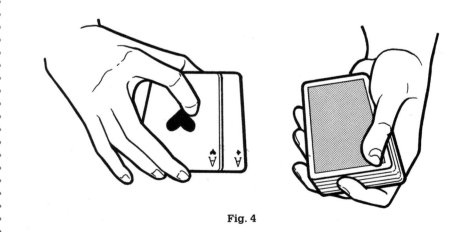

Fig. 4

★

STEP 11: At this point, you have successfully loaded a card in between the two aces. You can now proceed as the trick requires.

Double-decker Sandwich

E F F E C T

The deck is shuffled. The two red aces are removed and placed on the table. A card is selected. It is replaced in the deck. The performer then waves his hand over the two aces, and a face-down card appears in between them. The performer takes out this card and turns it face up. It is shown to be the selected card. The two aces are then placed face down back on the table and the selected card in the center of the deck. The magician spreads the deck on the table, and it is revealed that the selected card has again disappeared from the deck. He waves his hand over the aces, and a face-down card appears in between them. It is turned over and shown to be the selected card.

M E T H O D

STEP 1: Have the deck shuffled and the two red aces removed.

★

STEP 2: Pick up the aces and execute the "Classic Sandwich Technique," as described on page 88. It does not matter what the top card is.

★

STEP 3: This will leave you with one face-down card hidden between the two red aces. Now, you will give the aces an outward bend, making sure the face-down card stays square with the top ace (fig. 1).

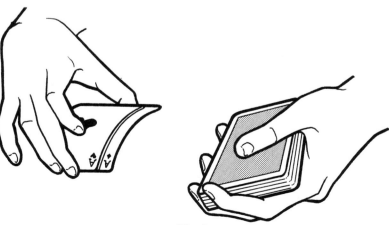

Fig. 1

N O T E
★

I was reading *Carneycopia,* a magic book by Stephen Minch and John Carney, when I came across a really neat trick, "Seconds on a Jack Sandwich." Though the idea of having a selected card appear sandwiched *twice* was innovative, the method involved palming a card in such a way that I was unable to do it because of my smaller hands. I devised this method as an alternative.

★

STEP 4: Now carefully place the "two" aces, as they are, on the table. Make sure the top ace and the card underneath don't spread. The concave bend will help (fig. 2).

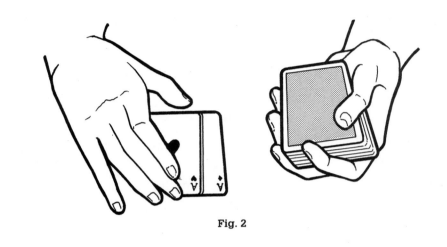

Fig. 2

★

STEP 5: Have a card selected. Execute the "To Control a Card to the Top of the Deck," as described on page 72. Pick up the deck and put it into left-hand mechanic's grip.

★

STEP 6: Bring your right hand over the cards on the table and make a magical gesture. (Do not let the hand come closer than half an inch from the cards.) Repeat this.

★

STEP 7: After repeating step 6, press the fingers of the right hand together and bring your hand all the way down on top of the cards resting on the table.

★

STEP 8: Press lightly on the cards. Spread out the fingers of the right hand, which will separate the top two cards of the packet on the table. It should look as if you just waved your hand over the two aces and a third card magically appeared between them, face down.

★

STEP 9: Now you will slide the face-down card to a position somewhere in front of the two aces. (The deck will still be in left-hand mechanic's grip.)

STEP 10: As you are sliding the card forward with your right hand, your left hand drops to your side with the deck. Your left thumb slightly pushes the top card over to the right. Under it, the left-hand pinkie applies pressure to the side of the deck right where it is. Holding the pinkie there, your thumb moves the card back to its original position, squared with the deck. You will now have a pinkie break under the top, selected, card.

★

STEP 11: Bring the left hand, holding the deck, to a comfortable position in front of you. You will now place the card currently on the table on top of the deck. After this, ask the spectator to name his card. Now, execute the "Double Lift," as described on page 74. It appears as if the selected card was the one that had appeared inside the two aces.

★

STEP 12: Turn the double back over, also described in the "Double Lift," but continue to apply pressure with your left-hand pinkie against the side of the deck so that you have a break under the top two face-down cards. Stick the top card into the deck, but protruding for half of its length (fig. 3), retaining a pinkie break under the top, selected card.

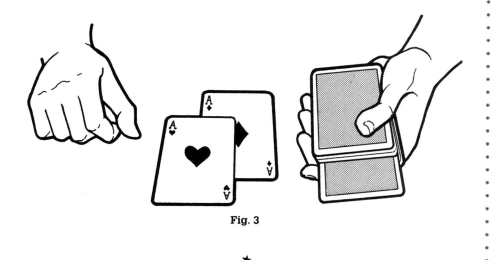

Fig. 3

★

STEP 13: Leaving the card protruding (which, by the way, the spectator thinks is his card), you pick up the aces and execute steps 4–10 of the "Classic Sandwich Technique," as described on page 88. You will find it is easily accomplished, even with the card sticking out from the center of the deck.

COMMENTS

★

This is a trick that you *must* practice in front of a mirror. That is the only way to make sure that the sandwiches don't *spread*. Make sure you handle this trick *crisply*. If you do, the trick will look *especially appetizing* to the audience. *Bon appétit!*

STEP 14: Repeat steps 3 and 4.

★

STEP 15: Push the card that is sticking out from the deck flush with it. Immediately spread the deck face up on the table, making sure not to disturb the sandwich cards, revealing that the selected card has vanished from the deck.

★

STEP 16: Now repeat steps 6–8, revealing a card face down between the two aces again. Ask the spectator to reach in and turn it over. It will be the previously selected card.

Coin and Currency Magic

he minting of coins goes back as far as the sixth century B.C., in Lydia, located in the area of modern-day Turkey. No one really knows when magicians first started using coins, but we do know that wandering entertainers in Europe often played for patrons' coins. It is probable that coin tricks first were created by those street performers.

Alexander Herrmann (1843–96), known as Herrmann the Great, would pick up a piece of fruit from a vendor's stand, cut it open, and find a $20 gold piece inside. Herrmann used this trick in the street markets of the town in which he was performing. Once the fruit merchant realized that it was a magician who stood before him, he would quickly spread the word that there was an incredible magic show in town. Presumably, ticket sales soared.

Peter Kougasian

Magician Peter M. Kougasian, an assistant district attorney in Manhattan, recalls one particularly memorable experience while performing at the Magic Towne House. The four-story building on Manhattan's East Side had magic performances every evening and children's matinees on the weekends. NBC-TV's *Tonight Show* host, Johnny Carson, then at the height of his fame, had made a reservation for a Friday evening in December 1983. It started snowing that afternoon, but Carson actually showed up. "Carson cracked up consistently through the show," Kougasian recalls. "To think, there I was doing the act I did every week, getting the laughs in the right places. But this time, it was Johnny Carson laughing. Every time he laughed, you could hear it. It was one of the most exciting things in my whole life. That was as good as it gets."

Currency magic broadened in popularity around the turn of the century with Thomas Nelson Downs's act, "The Miser's Dream." He would dazzle his audience by magically producing hundreds of coins from the air. Magicians still perform versions of this trick. Robert Torkova, winner of the Society of American Magicians' 1995 stage-magic contest, won the award with his version of this classic routine. Torkova is one of the few modern-day magicians who are able to do justice to this effect.

The late famous close-up conjurer Frank Garcia used to carry a peculiar looking coin. He called it his "37-cent coin." It was a half dollar coin with a wedge cut out of it that he judged was worth about 13 cents. Garcia used this coin for the incredible feat of making a borrowed coin apparently pass through a borrowed ring.

Possibly the most outstanding modern coin magician is David Roth, an accomplished pianist, who has lectured on coin magic before magic societies throughout the world. A book describing his work, *David Roth's Expert Coin Magic,* written by Richard Kaufman with Roth and widely heralded for its ground-breaking advance in the field, has recently been reprinted.

Among the reasons for the popularity of magic with currency is that coins are available in virtually every place, at almost any time. You can also practice coin magic wherever you go, inconspicuously. Because coins and bills are such familiar objects, magic with currency becomes all the more surprising to the audience.

Roll the Bills

Two bills of different denominations are shown. One bill is placed on top of the other, and the bills are rolled as one. When the bills are unrolled, with the spectator's fingers pinning down the ends of the bills, it is seen that the bill that had been on the bottom is now on the top, and vice versa.

STEP 1: Either take out or borrow two different bills. Ask a spectator which one he would like placed on top.

★

STEP 2: Place the bills in a "V" formation, with the one selected on top and to your left. The bottom bill should be pushed about an inch toward you (fig. 1, from the spectator's view, assuming a $5 bill was selected to be on top).

Fig. 1

I spent the summer of 1994 at the Buck's Rock summer camp in New Milford, Connecticut. I had heard that a magician, a former camper, was returning for a visit. I especially wanted to meet him because I had been out of contact with the world of magic (and the rest of the real world) for weeks. That's how I met Ben Robinson, a world-traveled professional magician and coauthor of the book *Twelve Have Died,* the definitive work on the famous and dangerous bullet catching trick.

We talked about mutual friends, exchanged snippets of gossip, and showed each other some tricks. One of the tricks he showed me, with bills, fooled me. That fall, we got together in New York at a deli where magicians gather. He mentioned, in passing, that the trick that had so impressed me was in *The Mark Wilson Complete Course in Magic.* This happened to be the first magic book I had ever purchased. I went home, hustled to the bookshelf, and learned that I had been fooled weeks earlier with an almost self-working trick. I later learned that the original version was created by Martin Crowe and first appeared in the May 1936 issue of *Jinx* magazine.

★

STEP 3: Now roll the bills toward the audience. First, begin rolling the bill on top, and then roll both of them together (fig. 2). Remind the spectators of the denomination of the bill that was on top.

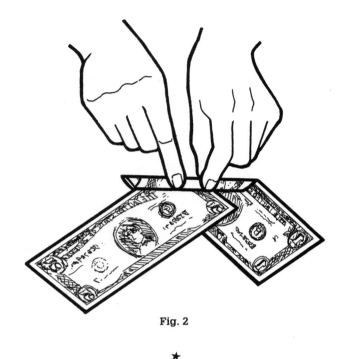

Fig. 2

★

STEP 4: As you are doing this, ask the spectator to cross his arms and extend his index fingers. Now, ask him to place his right index finger on the bill on his left and his left index finger on the bill on his right. Time this so that his hands are approaching the bills as you do the following move. When you reach the point when there is nothing left to see of the bottom bill but about an inch of the top bill (fig. 3), change the right hand's grip

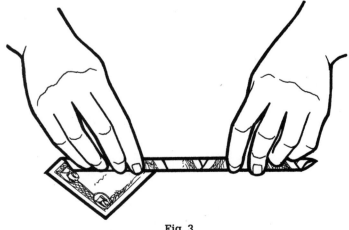

Fig. 3

on the bills, allowing the bottom bill to flip around the formation, brushing past your fingers in the process (fig. 4). This should be done right before the spectator's fingers touch the bills. His arms will hide the move from his line of sight and provide misdirection for anyone else watching.

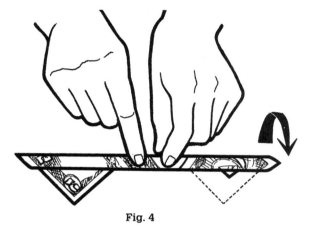

Fig. 4

★

STEP 5: Now there will be about an inch showing of each bill with the spectator's fingers of his crossed arms on top of them, as shown in fig. 5. Now, slowly unroll the bills. You will see that the top and bottom bills have mysteriously transposed.

Fig. 5

During a business trip to Latin America, banker/magician Alan Greenberg visited with the president of Argentina, for whom he did some magic. The country had just undergone a reevaluation of its currency. Greenberg congratulated the president on the change and then did a trick with the new Argentinean bills. During the remainder of his stay, Greenberg, accompanied by the president, visited many of the country's business centers. At virtually every stop, he was asked to do his bill trick.

The effect described below is most likely more elaborate than the trick performed by Greenberg in Argentina. However, it is an example of how a marvelous illusion can be created with the most common of objects—a dollar bill.

The Bill in Orange

EFFECT

Three oranges are sitting on the table. A $1 bill is borrowed from a spectator. The serial number is read off and written down. The bill is placed inside an envelope and the envelope is burned. Now, the spectator is asked to select one of the oranges, which is then cut open. There, inside the orange is the same $1 bill, with the same serial number.

PROPS

Three large navel oranges, with stems intact; two trays; an unsealed envelope with a piece of plain white paper the size of a dollar bill folded in eighths inside it; a cigarette lighter; pen and paper; tongs; a sharp knife; and two $1 bills.

PREPARATION

Most navel oranges come with labels on them. These are the type you should use. (The ones I use are large Sunkist oranges.) Remove the labels from two of the three oranges. The one with the label remaining is the one you will prepare. Before anything else, write down the bill's serial number. Next, with a small knife such as a Swiss Army knife, carefully pop off the little stem end on top of the orange with the label still on it (fig. 1). Take a sharpened wooden pencil and poke it, slowly, two-thirds

Fig. 1

of the way into the orange right where the stem end was (fig. 2). This will give you access to the inside of the orange. Take the bill and roll it up as tightly as possible. Then push it (fig. 3) inside the orange. When it is flush with the top of the orange, push the bill a little deeper into the orange with the eraser end of the pencil. Now take a dab of crazy glue and glue the little stem end back into place. You should not be able to tell that anything has been done to this orange. Place all three oranges on one of the trays. Write the serial number that you had written down before on your left index finger. (Or memorize it. Memorization is usually the route I take because it is possible for the spectators to see the serial number written on your finger. For the purposes of this explanation, however, I will assume you have written it on your finger). Place the lighter, a piece

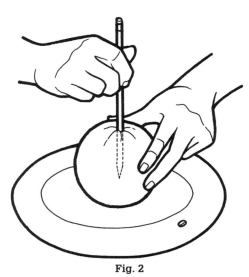

Fig. 2

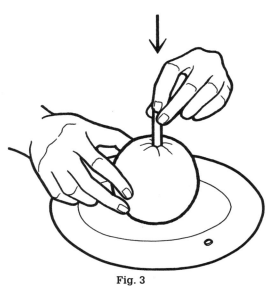

Fig. 3

of paper, and a pen inside your left pocket. Also place a second clean, fresh dollar bill inside your right pocket. You are now all set.

When you are ready to perform, have both trays side by side on the table, one with oranges, one with the tongs and the knife.

M E T H O D

STEP 1: First, you must borrow a clean, crisp dollar bill from a spectator. Next, go into your left pocket and pull out the pen and paper. Give these to the same spectator.

★

STEP 2: Pick up the bill and hold it, with index fingers on its face, others on its back, as shown in fig. 4. Tell the spectator that you will read off the serial number of the bill, and ask him to write it down. Pretend to read off the serial number of the bill, really reading the serial number written on your left index finger or reciting it from memory.

Fig. 4

★

STEP 3: Fold the borrowed bill into eighths, same as the paper inside the envelope. Pick up the envelope in your left hand and the folded bill in your right. Hold the bill between your thumb and index finger. Put all of your right-hand fingers inside the envelope, except for the thumb and index finger, which go behind it. Now clip the bill against the back of the envelope with your left thumb. It should look as if the bill is being placed inside the envelope. (Fig. 5 is a magician's view, fig. 6 is the audience's view.) Now, your left thumb pulls down on the bill so it goes into your left-hand finger palm (fig. 7).

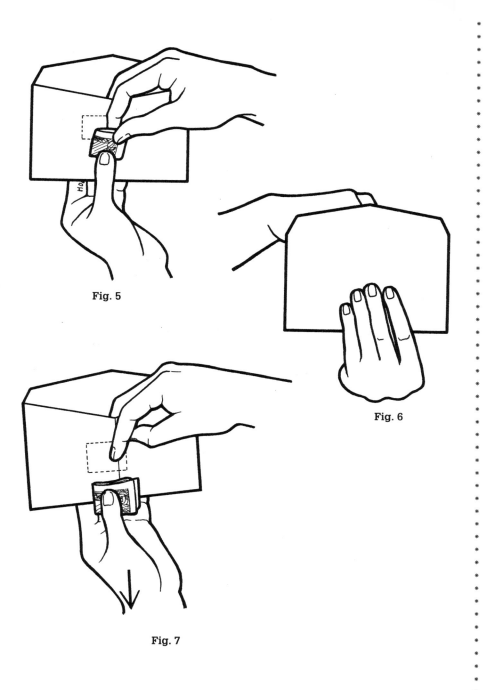

Fig. 5

Fig. 6

Fig. 7

★

STEP 4: Take the envelope in your right hand and, using your left hand, go back inside your left pocket and retrieve the lighter, leaving the folded bill behind. Put the lighter on the table. Now, seal the envelope. Pick up the tongs and hold them by their handles in your right hand. Put the envelope between the tongs and hold it over the empty tray. Pick up the lighter again. Before you light the envelope, hold the lighter behind the envelope for a few seconds. This will show a shadow of what the audience thinks is the bill (fig. 8). Now light the envelope.

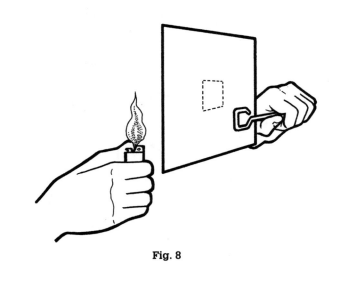

Fig. 8

★

STEP 5: Let the envelope burn to ash over the tray, being careful not to let anyone get too near the fire. When it is all done burning, use the tongs to break up the ash on the tray and put the tray and tongs aside. As far as the audience can tell, the dollar bill has been destroyed.

★

STEP 6: Now you are going to execute something called a "magician's choice." In effect, the spectator believes he is choosing between alternatives, when in fact he really has no choice in the matter at all. Let me explain.

You have the three oranges on the table. Have the spectator point to two of them. If one of the two is the orange with the label on it, we'll call that scenario 1. If there is no label on either of the two oranges, we'll call that scenario 2.

★

SCENARIO 1: Put the third orange, the one not selected, away. Ask the spectator to pick one of the remaining two. If he picks the one without the label on it, discard it and keep the other, saying, "This is the one we'll use." If he picks the one with the label on it, discard the other and keep the labeled orange. Either way, you end up with the spectator believing that he picked freely, when in fact he picked the prepared orange.

★

SCENARIO 2: Discard the two selected, saying, "Okay, that leaves us with this one." Once again, you end up with the prepared orange.

★

STEP 7: Have the spectator who originally loaned you the bill come up. Take the knife and cut the orange around its circumference, taking care not to disturb the rolled-up bill in its core (fig. 9). Now, have the spectator pull the two halves of the orange apart. Inside, he will find the rolled dollar (fig. 10). Take it out, slowly unroll it, and hold it in front of the spectator, asking him to read off the serial number of the bill one letter/number at a time, comparing it aloud with the number he wrote down earlier. Everyone will hear that the serial numbers match. So that the spectator need not deal with a wet, sticky bill, reach into your right pocket, pull out the fresh bill, and exchange it for the one from the orange.

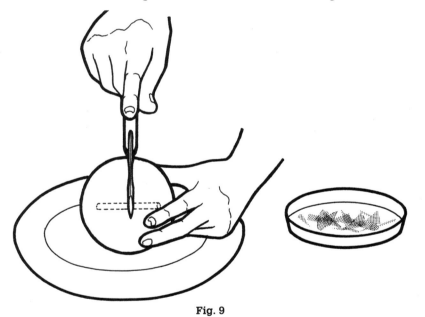

Fig. 9

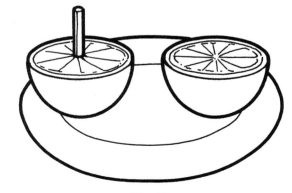

Fig. 10

The original version of this trick was popularized by comedic magician and famous strongman Emil Jarrow during the vaudeville era. In the early 1920s, when sawing a woman in half was popular, Jarrow, who did not perform the illusion, created a miniature alternative. He boldly advertised in a huge, building-sized banner, "SEE JARROW CUT A LEMON IN HALF." From all accounts, he was a fantastic magician. The late Al Flosso, whose magic store in New York City is still a popular magician's hangout, once said of Jarrow, "Who hasn't admired Jarrow's work? It is always a wonderful treat to see him perform on the stage or close-up. I never get tired watching him. He is and always will be my favorite."

A French magician named Alain Porthault, who performed under the name Diabolo, walked into a house to perform at a party in a very informal setting. He had a card selected and then took that card and ripped it into pieces. One of the pieces was given to a spectator. The others were made to disappear. Midway through the trick, Diabolo changed his mind and exclaimed, "Ah, I don't like this trick. I'm hungry. Please bring me a piece of fruit, and I will show you a miracle." An orange was brought to him. The orange was cut open and inside was found the selected card with a piece missing. It was the piece the spectator was holding. What the audience didn't know was that when Porthault had come in, he planted a prepared orange in the refrigerator. Using some of the principles described in the instructional text above and elsewhere in this book, he then made the card appear inside a *borrowed* piece of fruit.

I performed this effect for Bryant Gumbel and a national audience on NBC-TV's *Today* show on July 13, 1994. It was great fun. It is a highly visual, straightforward series of coin moves that will appeal to any audience.

As mentioned in the preface to this book, sleights are described immediately after the first trick in which they are used. Among the sleights used in "The Ambitious Coin" and whose descriptions follow are three important palming positions. These are vital components of the remaining coin tricks in this section. As a matter of fact, you should probably learn them before continuing, as knowing them while you learn the various sleights and tricks in this section will make life much easier.

The Ambitious Coin

EFFECT

A half-dollar coin is shown and placed in the performer's pocket with the right hand. The empty left hand reaches out and plucks the coin from the air. The right hand takes it and places it back in the pocket. An empty left hand once again plucks it from the air. This is repeated one last time, at which point the magician takes the half-dollar and makes it finally disappear.

METHOD

STEP 1: For this you need two half-dollars. Hold one in the right hand in classic palm and show the other one on your palm-up left hand. Now execute the "Shuttle Pass," as described on page 110, *apparently* transferring the coin from the left to the right hand.

★

STEP 2: The right hand now goes into the pocket to put the coin away. While it is there, however, what it really does is put the coin back into classic palm in the following manner: the coin is held at the fingertips and then shifted into fingertip rest. From there, curl the fingertips closer to the palm, putting the coin into position to be classic palmed. Now just push a little, and the coin is in. You can now remove your hand from your pocket as if the coin was left behind.

★

STEP 3: You will now show your *left* hand to be empty by what's known in magic as a "subtlety." In this case, it is a palm-down Ramsay subtlety, named after the great close-up magician John Ramsay. Curl your left middle, ring, and pinkie fingers over the coin and hold the index finger extended out and slightly curved, vaguely pointing (in the audience's direction) at what you say is an invisible coin. The audience will see most of the palm of your hand and believe that it is empty. The apparently empty palm should not be mentioned and only shown for a second or two (fig. 1).

★

STEP 4: Now turn the back of your left hand toward the audience and put the pad of your thumb against the coin. Using the pad of your thumb, push the coin to your fingertips, into view of the audience.

Fig. 1

★

STEP 5: Repeat steps 1–4 twice. The second time, really leave the coin in your pocket.

★

STEP 6: You now are dealing with only one coin. Transfer the coin to the right fingertips and execute the "Retention Vanish" (p. 111) in which the coin ends up in fingertip rest. To get the coin into classic palm, simply do the move described in step 2. When you next have occasion to go into your pocket, leave the coin there.

Sleight of hand with coins is the hardest thing you will learn in this book. It requires quite a bit of practice but is a fantastic form of magic. Also, the transfer from fingertip rest to classic palm described in step 2 is used in many of the routines that follow, so make sure that you learn how to do it.

Palming (the concealment of an object in one's hand) is the basis of almost all sleight-of-hand coin magic, as is the control of a card in card magic. Make sure you have mastered these palms before you go on because every coin trick in this section uses at least one of these three sleights. Two of these, classic palm and fingertip rest, need only be learned in your dominant hand; the third, finger palm, must be learned by both hands. I recommend starting out by learning them all in your dominant hand.

Palming

Classic Palm

A coin in classic palm is held between the flesh at the base of the thumb and the heel of the hand. For now, to get the feel of it, just shove it in there with the other hand. This palm position, though the most difficult, is also the most convincing. All fingers can be spread casually, and, given practice, the hand can look natural (figs. 1 and 2).

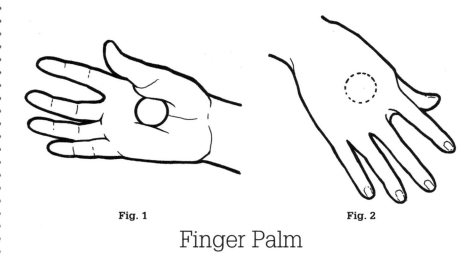

Fig. 1   **Fig. 2**

Finger Palm

This also can be a convincing way of palming a coin. In "The Ambitious Coin," a sleight is taught that enables you to show the palm of your hand empty while finger palming a coin. In this position, the coin is held by the middle and ring fingers, between the base crease of your fingers and in between the top and the middle crease. The index and pinkie fingers are free and can just be slightly curved like the middle and ring fingers (figs. 3 and 4) or can be used to point (figs. 5 and 6).

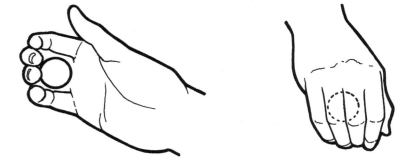

Fig. 3   **Fig. 4**

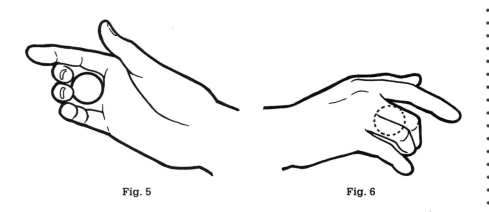

Fig. 5   Fig. 6

Fingertip Rest

This is not exactly a palm, but it is a way to conceal a coin. It is just what the name implies, a rest or intermediate position on the way to a palm. The hand is curled with the fingertips about two inches from the palm of the hand. The coin just rests on these fingertips (fig. 7).

Fig. 7

Harry Anderson

Among TV's best-known characters was Judge Harold T. Stone, presiding over his *Night Court* with humor and compassion. Judge Stone was played by Harry Anderson, who started in show business as a street magician. His career as a television performer thrives while he continues to contribute to magic by creating some of the best tricks in the magic repertory. Perhaps the most widely known of these is the "Mismade Bill," in which the face of a dollar bill is magically rearranged.

Shuttle Pass

METHOD

STEP 1: One half-dollar is classic palmed in your right hand, another is displayed on your left hand's fingertips. Curl the right-hand fingers inward to a loose fist. As the audience's attention is drawn to the left hand, let the coin fall from right classic palm to your right fingertip rest.

★

STEP 2: Adjust the coin on your left hand so that it is right over the part of your fingers where you would finger palm a coin. This is called open finger palm.

★

STEP 3: This step and the next require a flowing rhythm. First, begin to bring your hands together.

★

STEP 4: When they get about an inch away from each other, two things must happen simultaneously: (1) turn your left hand over, finger palming the coin as you do so; and (2) turn your right hand palm up and, at the same time, straighten out your right fingers (fig.1). If done properly, the coin in the right hand will stay on the pads of your right fingertips and not fall to your palm or to the floor. The sequence will look as if you have transferred the coin from one hand to the other.

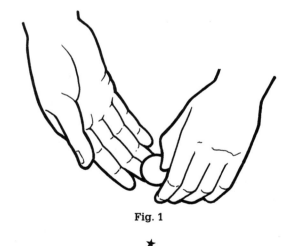

Fig. 1

★

STEP 5: Now, put your thumb on the exposed coin and rotate your hand to display the coin. At the same time, slowly drop your left hand to your side.

Retention Vanish

M E T H O D

STEP 1: Hold a half-dollar between your right index and middle fingers and your thumb. Hold your left hand palm up in front of you.

★

STEP 2: Bring the right hand on to the left hand, as depicted in fig. 1. Begin to close your left fingers over the coin and right fingers.

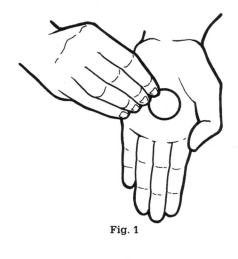

Fig. 1

★

STEP 3: By the time the pinkies of your right and left hands touch in the process of closing your left hand, the left hand fingers will be at an approximate 90° angle with the left palm, and the coin should be out of view. It is not until this point that you do "the move." Your right index finger and thumb keep a good grip on the coin. However, your middle, ring, and pinkie fingers straighten out and cover the coin (fig. 2 is a magician's view, fig. 3 an audience's view).

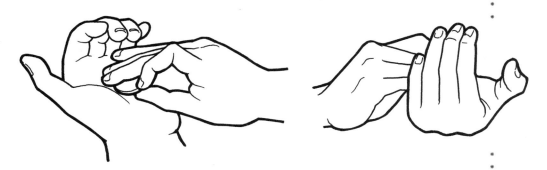

Fig. 2   **Fig. 3**

N O T E
★
An early version of this coin vanish was described in *Greater Magic* by John Northern Hilliard, published in 1938, one of the great compendiums of modern magic. The vanish in *Greater Magic* was credited to Thomas J. Crawford and was called "The Elusive Coin Pass." This move was updated and popularized by expert coin magician David Roth. It is the most visually deceptive vanish of a coin I know. It is not difficult, but it does require good timing.

★

STEP 4: Meanwhile, your left fingers continue to close over the "coin." Your right index finger now lets go of the coin. At the same time, all the other right-hand fingers curl inward, bringing the coin into fingertip rest (fig. 4). At this point, the left hand closes completely as the right hand moves away (fig. 5) and drops to your side.

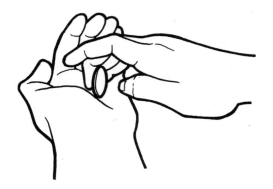

Fig. 4

Fig. 5

★

STEP 5: With your right hand, execute the move taught in step 2 of "The Ambitious Coin," as described on page 106, transferring the coin into classic palm. With your left hand, slowly make a crumpling motion, finally opening it to reveal the disappearance.

Coins to Glass

N O T E
★

Any glass will work for this trick. I prefer to use either a double shot glass or a small juice glass because of their manageable size.

E F F E C T

Two coins and a glass rest on the table. The magician picks up one of the coins and makes it visually penetrate through the bottom of the glass. The second coin, however, is made to fly invisibly through the air, finally landing, with a "clink," inside the glass.

M E T H O D

STEP 1: Two half-dollars lie on the table; the glass rests mouth up to the right of the coins. With your right hand, pick up one of the coins and execute the "Retention Vanish," as described on page 111. The left hand remains closed.

★

STEP 2: Holding the coin in classic palm in your right hand, pick up the glass by its mouth with the tips of your right-hand fingers circling the rim (fig. 1).

Fig. 1

★

STEP 3: Now, take your left hand, open it, and immediately hit its palm against the bottom of the glass (fig. 2). At the same time, release the coin from right-hand classic palm. If these two actions are done simultaneously, it will look to the audience as if the coin penetrated the bottom of the glass. Put the glass, coin still within, on to the table.

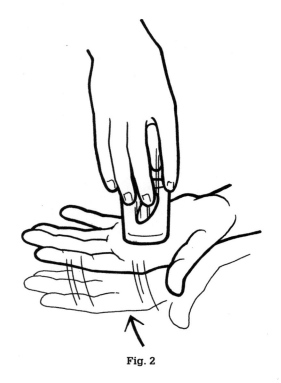

Fig. 2

★

STEP 4: Pick up the second coin and execute the "Drop Vanish" (page 116). Keep the left hand closed. Casually execute the Ramsay subtlety as described in step 3 of "The Ambitious Coin," on page 106. Pick up the glass by the rim with your right index finger in front and your thumb in the rear. The remaining fingers are slightly curled, holding the finger-palmed coin (fig. 3).

★

STEP 5: Now, open your left hand as you pretend to throw the nonexistent coin into the air. Pause a beat or two and then release the coin from right-hand finger palm, letting it fall into the glass.

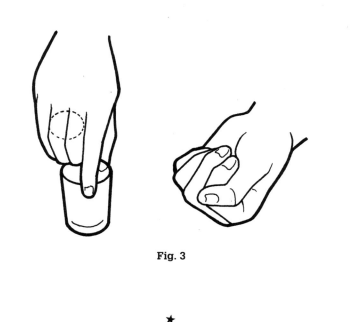

Fig. 3

★

STEP 6: Place the glass on the table and let what you have just done sink in.

For this trick and others, I decided that a heavy-duty two-ounce shot glass with a thick, recessed bottom was the glass I needed. Like the surfer looking for the perfect wave, I have been searching for the perfect shot glass. The shot glass I needed was not the type normally found in your local gift shop or department store. So I hit the streets. Going from bartender to bartender, I explained (well, stretching the truth a little) that I collected shot glasses and asked if I could see the shot glass they used. A little awkward for a thirteen-year-old barely tall enough to see over the bar and definitely not old enough to be served at one. The bartender would show me the glass he used, and if it was the type I liked, I would offer to buy it. Every bartender I asked smiled and said I could keep it.

I now have a large collection of shot glasses. These days, whenever I inquire about one, I'm telling the absolute truth when I say I'm a collector.

C O M M E N T S

★

This move takes only about a second. It is not a series of separate actions but rather one flowing movement, executed casually.

Drop Vanish

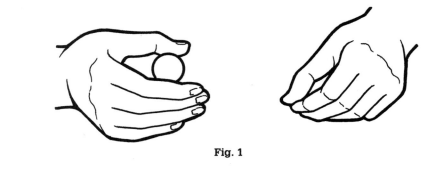

M E T H O D

STEP 1: The right hand holds a coin by its edges, between the thumb and index finger (fig. 1).

Fig. 1

★

STEP 2: Your left hand is brought, palm up, about six inches below your right hand. Now, the two hands come together, at which point the actual move takes place.

★

STEP 3: The right thumb relaxes, letting the coin fall. At the same time, the right hand tilts forward slightly, causing the coin to fall into right-hand finger palm, rather than into the left hand (figs. 2 and 3).

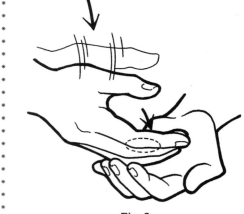

Fig. 2

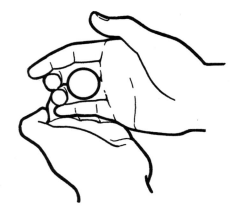

Fig. 3

★

STEP 4: At this point, your right fingers curl inward, finger palming the coin. Simultaneously, your left fingers begin to close, as the left hand moves down and forward (figs. 4 and 5).

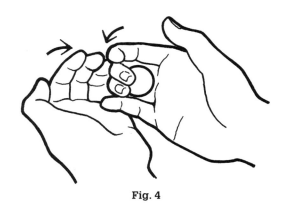

Fig. 4

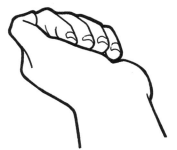

Fig. 5

Coins Across

E F F E C T

Four coins are shown and placed in the right hand, which closes into a fist over them. The left hand is also closed into a fist. The magician makes a magical tossing action from one hand to the other, opening his hands to show only three coins in the right and one in the left. The hands are closed again, the action is repeated, and now there are two coins in each hand. This is repeated once more, leaving one coin in the right hand and three in the left. Finally, the three coins are placed into a spectator's hand, and the fourth coin is placed into the magician's hand. The magical action is made, and all four coins are found to be in the spectator's hand and none in the magician's.

M E T H O D

STEP 1: You need five half-dollars for this trick. One is classic palmed in the right hand; the others are displayed on the palm of the left hand. Make sure the bottom coin is at the base of the fingers, directly in position to be finger palmed. Now, execute the "Utility Switch," as described on page 122, leaving you with one coin finger palmed in the left hand and four displayed in the right hand. Make sure the bottom coin on the right hand is in open classic palm, in position to be classic palmed (fig. 1). Close both hands into fists, turning them both palm down as you do. As you do this, classic palm the bottom coin of the four coins in the right hand.

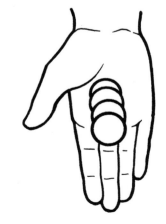

Fig. 1

★

STEP 2: Now, make an action as if you were throwing a coin from your right hand to the left invisibly. Drop the one coin from your left hand onto the table, pause, and drop three from your right, leaving the last one in classic palm.

★

STEP 3: With your left hand, pick back up the coin you just dropped out of it. Execute the "Shuttle Pass," as described on page 110, leaving a coin hidden in left finger palm and one displayed on the right fingertips. You will now perform a *palm-up* Ramsay subtlety with your left hand, like the palm-down one described in step 3 of "The Ambitious Coin," on page 106. The difference here is that the hand is palm up, yet the fingers still curl over the coin, showing most of the left hand to be empty. Now, simply put the coin from the right hand on to the left palm (fig. 2). Quickly close the left hand, the fingertips pressing against the back edge of the coin resting on the palm, and retaining the other coin in finger palm. This prevents the two coins from hitting each other and clinking.

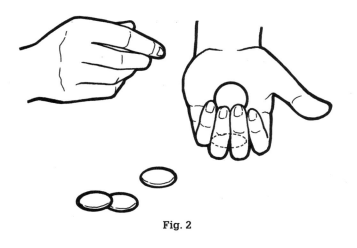

Fig. 2

★

STEP 4: Now pick up the other three coins with your right hand and display them, once again making sure the bottom coin is in open classic palm. Close the right hand, turning it over, and palming the bottom coin as you do so, in the same fashion as in step 1. Make the magical gesture and drop two coins from the left hand onto the table and then two from the right hand, retaining the third in classic palm.

★

STEP 5: Now, pick up the two left-hand coins with the left hand and execute a "Utility Switch," leaving one coin finger palmed in the left hand and two displayed in the right hand. Toss the two coins from the right hand back into the left, being careful not to let the audience see the finger-palmed coin. Close the left hand over all three of the coins. Finally, pick up the two right-hand coins and display them, making sure the bottom one is in open classic palm. Close the right hand over the two coins, classic palming the bottom one as the hand is turned over. Make a magical gesture and then drop the three from the left hand and one from the right hand, retaining the last coin in right-hand classic palm.

★

STEP 6: At this point, you will have one coin classic palmed in your right hand. With your right hand, pick up the three that are in a group on the table. Shake the coins a little so they clink against each other, and secretly allow the coin that had been classic palmed to drop to the stack of three coins. Ask a spectator to extend his hand. Place the stack of three (really four) coins in his hand and quickly close his hand over the coins without letting him see that there are four coins there (figs. 3, 4, and 5). Rotate his fist so that his clenched fingers are face down, an additional precaution against him opening the hand prematurely.

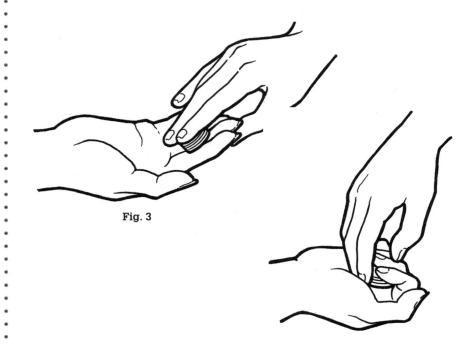

Fig. 3

Fig. 4

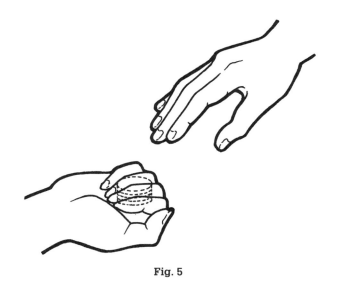

Fig. 5

★

STEP 7: Take the last coin and execute the "Retention Vanish." Now ask the spectator to open his hand, revealing four coins.

Executed correctly, this trick is one of the most magical routines you can do. Make sure to practice the last sequence with relatives and friends.

There is a different trick, known as "Coins Through the Table," that can be executed almost exactly the same way as "Coins Across." On each step, simply bring your left hand under the table and your right hand over the top. Now slap your right hand on top of the table, dropping all except the palmed coin. Bring your left hand out, palm up, showing that a coin has apparently penetrated. You can repeat this for the next two coins. You can still use the spectator's hand at the end; just bring his hand under the table. While the method stays almost exactly the same, the trick is very different. In "Coins Across," the effect is that coins go invisibly from hand to hand. In "Coins Through the Table," the coins go through the tabletop.

Utility Star Switch

METHOD

STEP 1: We'll assume that you are dealing with five coins, one of which is to be kept hidden, as is the case with "Coins Across." Start with one coin classic palmed in the right hand and four displayed on the left palm, the bottom one in open finger palm, that is, directly in position to be finger palmed (fig. 1).

Fig. 1

★

STEP 2: Now move your left hand up a few inches. Toss all but the bottom coin of the coins in the left hand on to the right hand. The bottom one is finger palmed as you toss (fig. 2). This will show four coins on the right palm (fig. 3).

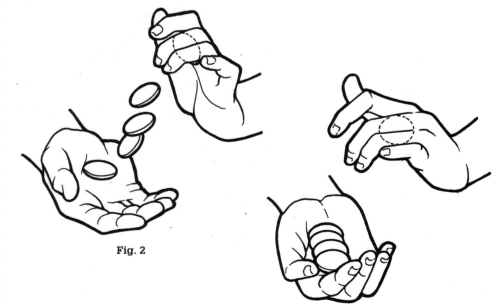

Fig. 2

Fig. 3

Ball Magic

Perhaps because we live on a spherical planet and are enchanted by a full moon, the use of spherical objects by fortune tellers, jugglers, and magicians just sort of makes sense.

Indian street magicians, called *jadoo wallah,* performed cups and balls for British travelers in the early eighteenth century. The cups they used had small handles extending upward from the bottoms of the inverted cups. This made it easy for them to lift the cups with the webbing between their fingers. The travelers were sure that the small handles somehow concealed the balls that had disappeared. Actually, the ancient device helped the jadoo wallah quicken their performance, and nothing more.

Max Malini (1873–1942), "The Last of the Mountebanks," had a reputation for making baseballs appear in his unusually small hands.

Malini was the first person to perform the cups and balls as impromptu close-up magic. As a matter of fact, Malini was so adept at the art that he would often do the cups and balls with nothing more than three glass tumblers wrapped in newspaper, using plump cherries rather than balls. As a grand finale, he would lift up the tumblers to reveal three large pieces of fruit.

A Danish vaudeville magician of the 1920s, Clement de Lion, played an important role in the development of the classic multiplying billiard-ball trick. He produced the balls between his fingers and made them change color. At the time, his billiard-ball act was a great novelty, and de Lion was invited to perform before European royalty and in theaters throughout the world.

As you will see in the tricks that follow, there are a wide variety of effects that can be performed with balls. Reginald Scot said in his 1584 book, *The Discouerie of Witchcrafte,* "Concerning the ball, the plaies and devices therewith are infinite inasmuch as if you can handle them well, you may show therewith a hundred feats."

The Cups and Balls

Most of the tricks in this book can be done with things you can find around the house. In this case, though some conventional beverage cups will work for this trick, it is best that you purchase from a magic shop a set of cups specifically designed for a cups and balls routine. A plastic set (balls included) can cost as little as $5. A step up would be a set of aluminum cups, costing up to $25. A handsome copper set can cost more, depending on the size of the cups and the weight of the copper. The two qualities most important for the cups are a recessed bottom (fig. 1) and a stacking ridge to leave room for the balls when the cups are stacked (fig. 2). In addition to the cups and the balls, you will also need a set of "sponge balls" (the orange balls discussed in the *Effect*), which cost under $5 and are also available from your local magic shop.

N O T E
★

The cups and balls is one of the oldest tricks in magic. There are references to it as far back as 2500 B.C., on the walls of an Egyptian tomb. The Greek writer Alciphron wrote of the trick in third century A.D. Not only is it one of the oldest effects in magic, it is also one of the most beautiful.

Johnny "Ace" Palmer won the title of World Champion Magician and the coveted Grand Prix, in 1988, in Holland. It was the first time that the award of Grand Prix had gone to a close-up magician. A feature of his act was his cups and balls routine, climaxed by the production of live baby chicks.

Bill Tarr, magician and sculptor, believes that "the reason the cups and balls have persisted for thousands of years is because they are a work of art."

Albert S. Galton, a regional sales manager for a major food company, uses the cups and balls to attract attention at trade shows and other business events.

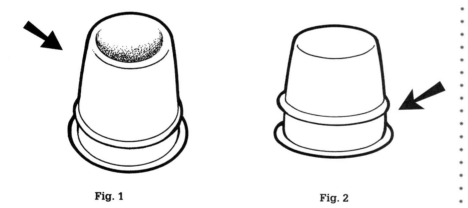

Fig. 1   **Fig. 2**

Two additional notes: Where I refer to a ball being palmed, I mean palmed basically the same way a coin would be finger palmed. A description of a coin finger palm can be found in "Palming," on page 108. Just adapt that technique to balls. Finally, virtually throughout the routine, the cups are inverted, that is, mouth down, bottom up.

This routine is probably the most complex in this book. It will take time to memorize and perfect. Should you like to do the cups and balls without spending the time required to learn the full routine presented below, you can perform the routine just through step 5. Up until that point, no sleight of hand is required.

EFFECT

Three small balls and three cups are shown. The performer then shows how the balls can go through the cups, jump around, disappear, reappear, and so on. Finally, the cups are lifted and three large orange balls are revealed.

SETUP

Three of the sponge balls are in your right pocket. The cups are stacked on the table, mouth up. In the top cup lie three of the small balls. Between the bottom two lies the secret fourth.

METHOD

STEP 1: The cups are lifted and are held by the left hand at the side of the stack and the right hand at the bottom (fig. 3). The right hand pulls down on the bottom cup, freeing it from the stack, and rapidly turns the cup over and on to the center of the mat or performance area (figs. 4 and 5). This should be done fairly quickly so the secret ball stays in the cup, but not jerkily, so as to arouse suspicion. The cup you just set down is now at what we will call "Position B." The current bottom cup of the stack is now pulled away. At about the same rate as the first, turn this cup over and on to the right of the performance area. We will call this "Position C." Finally, take the last cup and carefully pour out the three balls. Now, put it on to the left, "Position A."

Fig. 3

Fig. 4

Fig. 5

Sequence A

STEP 2: The balls are arranged in a horizontal row, one in front of each cup. The ball in front of the cup at "Position B" is placed on top of that cup. The cup at "Position C" at the performer's right is now lifted and placed on top of the "Position B" cup. Finally, the "Position A" cup is placed on top of all. A magical gesture is made and the stacked cups are lifted together, apparently showing that the ball has penetrated the bottom cup. Turn the stack mouth up.

★

STEP 3: The cups are now separated and placed mouth down, one at a time, from right to left, with the center cup on top of the ball at "Position B" on the table. This is done in the same manner as in step 1. If this is done fairly rapidly, no one will know that there are really two balls under the "Position B" cup.

★

STEP 4: Now place the ball on the right on top of the "Position B" cup. Then stack the other two cups on top of that. Make a magical gesture. Lift the stack, revealing that the second ball has penetrated. Turn the stack mouth up.

★

STEP 5: Repeat step 3, this time leaving three balls under the center cup. Repeat step 4 with the last ball.

Sequence B

STEP 6: Arrange the balls in a horizontal, A-B-C row again, one at left, one at center, and one on the right. Fairly rapidly lay out the cups from right to left, behind the balls, mouth down. This will leave a secret, extra ball under the "Position B" cup. Pick up the visible ball at the center, and execute the "Ball Vanish," as described on page 134. Now, with your left hand, pick up the center cup, revealing the secret ball. It will seem, astonishingly, that you have made a ball vanish and magically reappear under the cup. While the audience's attention is drawn to the just revealed ball, the cup is handed from the left to the right hand, holding the mouth of the cup right above the palmed ball, in preparation for the "Ball Load," as described on page 136 (fig. 6).

★

STEP 7: Place the cup in your right hand on top of the just revealed ball at center, executing the "Ball Load" with the ball in your hand at the same time.

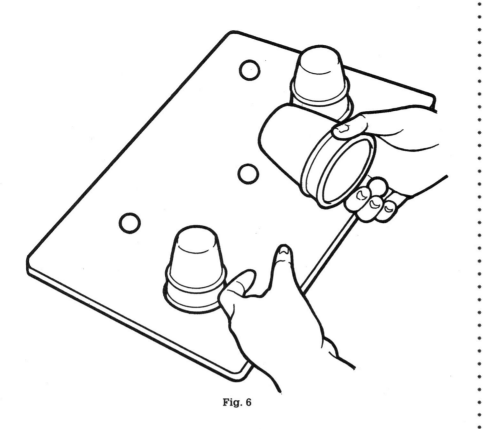

Fig. 6

★

STEP 8: Pretend to cover the ball on the right with the "Position C" cup, really executing the "Ball Steal," page 137, as you do so.

★

STEP 9: Finally, place the "Position A" cup on top of the remaining visible ball on the left, at the same time executing the "Ball Load." This last cross-reach to the left side with your right hand can be awkward. However, it can be more easily accomplished if you reach behind the cups rather than in front or over them. Your current position is this: There are no balls under the "Position C" cup. There are two balls each under both "Position A and B" cups. Make a magical gesture, and lift up the cup at "Position C" revealing the disappearance of a ball. Leave this cup on its side, mouth facing the audience. Now ask the spectator to pick one of the remaining cups. Whichever one he selects, lift it up, revealing two balls. Leave this cup on its side. Pick up one of these two balls.

★

STEP 10: Execute the "Ball Vanish." Pick up the remaining cup, revealing two balls. Place this cup back down, but not onto one of the visible balls.

Instead, execute the "Ball Load" with the ball that is palmed in your right hand (fig. 7). You are set for Sequence C.

Fig. 7

Sequence C

STEP 11: If you are working on a close-up pad, tuck one of the balls under the front edge of the pad. If you are not, simply place one of the visible balls aside. At this point, arrange the cups, mouth down, in a horizontal row. The one with the secret ball under it must be moved to "Position B." Now, with your right hand, take one of the visible balls and apparently place it into your right pocket. Really, you secretly palm it in your right hand.

★

STEP 12: Bring out your right hand, with the palmed ball, and lift up the "Position A" cup by its bottom ridge with the right hand (fig. 8). Use this cup to tap the top of the two other cups. As you do this, you execute a type of ball load, as follows. As you tap the first cup, your fingers extend next to the mouth of the cup (fig. 9). From this position, simply let the ball roll off your fingers into the cup. Retract your fingers as you tap the second cup.

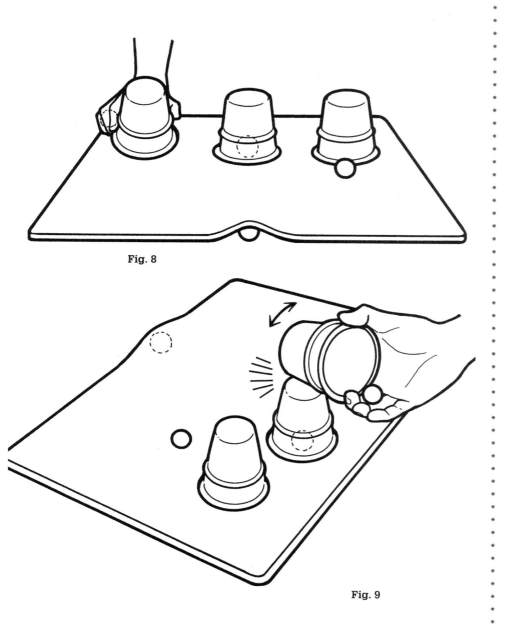

Fig. 8

Fig. 9

★

STEP 13: Take the cup you are holding and rapidly rotate it mouth down, as you place it on top of the "Position B" cup. This will leave you with one ball under the bottom cup of the "Position B" stack and one ball under the top cup of the "Position B" stack, with one cup left in "Position C."

★

STEP 14: Take the remaining visible ball and pretend to place it in your right pocket, once again palming it. Pick up the "Position C" cup and repeat the "Ball Load" described in step 12, only this time do it as you gesture toward the ball under the edge of the mat or placed aside. Finally, place it on top of the "Position B" stack as described in step 13.

★

STEP 15: Now retrieve the ball that is under the mat or had been placed aside. Using this ball, execute the "Miller Penetration," as described on page 138, with the top cup. When you are finished, the audience's attention will be directed at the ball now atop the stack. Take the cup you are holding in your left hand with your right hand and place it at "Position C," executing the "Ball Load" with the palmed ball as you do so. Lift up the ball on top of the "Position B" stack and repeat the "Miller Penetration." Transfer the cup to the right hand and place it at "Position A," loading the ball as you do so. Repeat this sequence with the last cup, leaving it at "Position B" with the palmed ball loaded underneath it. This will leave you with one ball visible on the table.

Sequence D

STEP 16: Take this ball with your right hand and place it in your pocket. This time you really do leave it there. This time, however, you palm one of the sponge balls in your pocket with your right hand.

★

STEP 17: With your left hand, lift the cup at "Position C," revealing that one of the balls has returned. Transfer the cup to your right hand and put the cup back down behind the just-revealed ball, loading the sponge ball as you do so. Load the sponge ball exactly as you would the smaller regular ball. Pick up the regular ball and place it in your pocket, grabbing a sponge ball while there. Lift up the "Position B" cup with your left hand, revealing that a second ball has returned. Transfer the cup to the right hand and place it back down behind the just revealed ball, again loading the sponge ball. Put the small ball in your pocket and leave it there, grabbing a sponge ball in its place. Lift up the "Position A" cup with your left hand, revealing that the last ball has returned. For the third time, transfer the cup to the right hand, and place the cup back down, behind the just-revealed ball, loading the sponge ball under it. Take the last small ball and place it in your pocket, leaving it there.

★

STEP 18: You must now build up what you are about to do. Let's just think about what's going on in the spectator's mind. He is thinking, "What's going to happen next with these shiny cups and these little balls?" The silent answer might be, "Well, I bet the little balls are going to jump back under the cups again." He can't even fathom the possibility of larger, different colored balls appearing under the cups. So, step a couple of feet away from the cups, pause, go back, and lift up the cups, revealing the sponge balls to a sea of applause.

C O M M E N T S
★

This routine is in my working repertoire. It has been audience tested, and, I think I can say, audience approved. Once you have command of the sleights involved, you can create a routine of your own, and I encourage you to do so.

Also, there is something to be said for making all of the moves in this routine flow smoothly. If you can do that, the somewhat elongated pause before the revelation has more of an impact on the audience.

Ball Vanish

STEP 1: Hold the ball in your right hand, between your thumb and index finger (fig. 1). Bring your left hand directly under your right hand (fig. 2).

Fig. 1

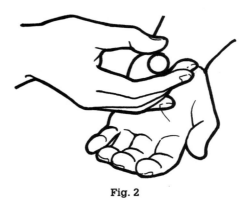

Fig. 2

★

STEP 2: Relax your right thumb, allowing the ball to roll down your fingers. When it is directly in between the ring and middle fingers of your right hand, curl them inward, finger palming the ball (figs. 3 and 4).

★

STEP 3: Close your left hand into a fist as it moves up and away from your right hand (fig. 5). It will appear to the spectator as if the ball was dropped into the left hand.

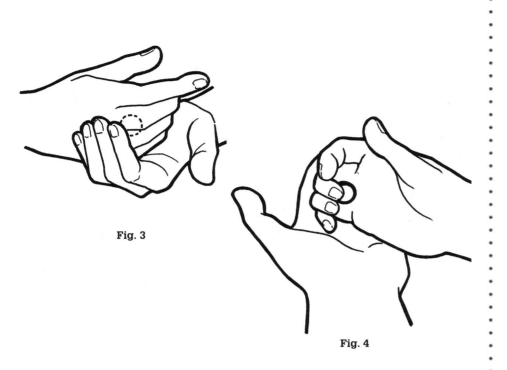

Fig. 3

Fig. 4

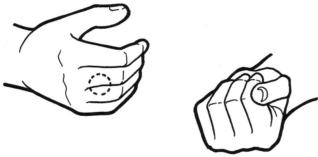

Fig. 5

★

STEP 4: Now, make a crumpling motion with your left hand, finally revealing that the ball has vanished.

Ball Load

STEP 1: Let's say you have one ball finger palmed in your right hand. You want to load this ball beneath the cup you are holding in the same hand (fig. 1).

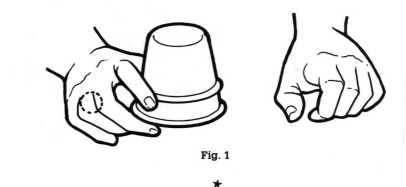

Fig. 1

★

STEP 2: To load the ball, you move to place the cup down. Right after the front edge of the cup has hit the table, and before the back edge has, extend your right fingers, letting the ball roll under the cup. Retract your fingers and put the back edge down (figs. 2–4). You have loaded the ball.

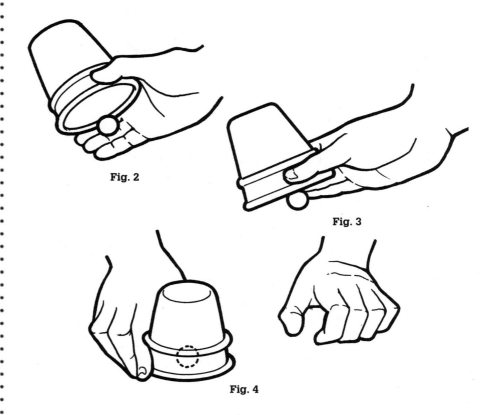

Fig. 2

Fig. 3

Fig. 4

Ball Steal

METHOD

STEP 1: You are holding a cup in your right hand, gripping it at the rim, between the index finger and thumb. You intend to place the mouth of the cup over the ball, but your real intention is to steal the ball as you cover it with the cup.

★

STEP 2: When you are ready to put the cup down, extend your ring finger under the mouth of the cup (fig. 1). Right after the front edge has touched the table, but before the back edge has, the move takes place. Your ring finger curls in front of the ball and rolls it back against the palm (figs. 2–4). The ball is held between the ring finger and palm. Put down the back edge of the cup. The entire move takes a split second. From its initial position, the ball can be easily maneuvered into a finger palm.

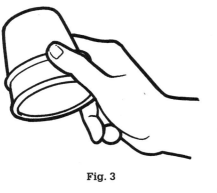

Fig. 1

Fig. 2

Fig. 3

Fig. 4

NOTE

★

This move was created by the late close-up genius Charlie Miller. His work contributed significantly to making modern-day close-up magic a major component of the art.

This description involves only two cups, making the move less complicated to learn. In the routine, however, the number of cups used in the move will vary.

Miller Penetration

METHOD

STEP 1: Let's assume you have two cups, stacked one upon the other, with a secret ball between them. The ball that you are going to do the move with rests visibly on top of the top cup. Pick up this ball with your left hand, as your right hand closes into a fist. Rest your right fist on the top cup (fig. 1). Now, take the ball with your left hand and place it atop the fist (fig. 2). Your left hand now holds onto the top cup around the stacking ridge (fig. 3).

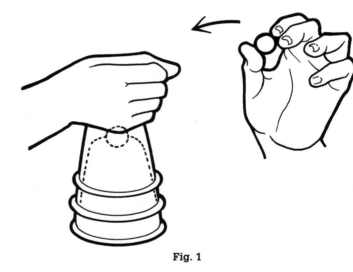

Fig. 1

Fig. 2

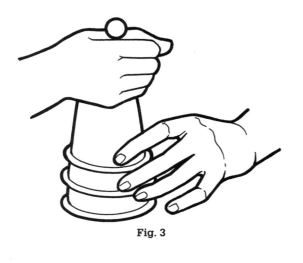

Fig. 3

★

STEP 2: Okay, here's the move. Simultaneously, these two actions happen: (1) your right hand will open up slightly, allowing the ball to fall into the fist (fig. 4), and (2) your left hand lifts the top cup, as your right hand remains on top of it, revealing the ball under it (fig. 5). It will appear as if the ball simply penetrated the top cup. You will be left with a ball palmed in the left hand, which you may use in a subsequent move or dispose of, depending on the routine you are following.

Fig. 4

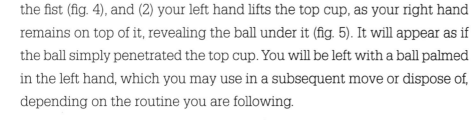

Fig. 5

COMMENTS

★

David Williamson, a creative and talented magician from Virginia, suggests that if you are working on a close-up mat, you should tilt the stack of cups forward slightly just before you do the move (fig. 6). This way, when the cup is lifted to reveal the hidden ball, the ball is moving and appears as if it had just arrived.

Fig. 6

Sponge Balls

E F F E C T

The magician magically produces a single sponge ball. It disappears, reappears, and finally multiplies into two balls. These balls perform some magical feats before they multiply again into three. More magical feats, and finally, they all disappear.

P R O P S

Back again to the magic shop. You need a set of four sponge balls. (They shouldn't cost more than $5.) Actually, these are the same balls you use for final loads in the cups and balls routine elsewhere in this section of the book.

Sponge balls facilitate many different tricks because they are readily compressible. They can be gripped easily and securely. You can make two or three look as though they were one, palm them quite easily, and so on.

M E T H O D
Sequence A

STEP 1: Start out with two sponge balls in your right pocket, one in your left pocket, and one palmed (fig. 1) in your right hand. Ask a spectator to help you with the trick. Ask him to extend his left hand. Your right hand grips his left hand, palm up, from below, secretly holding the ball be-

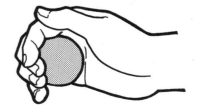

Fig. 1

tween the back of his left hand and the fingers of your right hand (fig. 2). Because of the texture of the sponge ball, the spectator will not feel it against the back of his hand.

Fig. 2

★

STEP 2: Now your left hand mimes the action of plucking something from the air. You then claim that the invisible ball is going to penetrate the spectator's hand. Pretend to push it through the spectator's hand. Ask him if he felt anything. The response will be negative. Then, very slowly, draw out the sponge ball from beneath the spectator's hand.

★

STEP 3: You can now do a little improvisation. Make the ball disappear, using the "Sponge-Ball Retention Vanish," as described on page 145; make it reappear from beneath your elbow, and so on.

★

STEP 4: Finally, execute the "Sponge-Ball Retention Vanish." Reach into your right pocket and pull out a second ball (keeping the original ball palmed in your right hand), explaining that the ball traveled to your pocket.

Sequence B

STEP 5: Lay the visible ball on the table. Ask the spectator to extend his hand again. With your right hand, pick up the ball from the table, adding it to the palmed ball. Squeeze the two balls together so that they look like one ball (figs. 3 and 4). Put them both in the spectator's hand and close his hand on them. Pretend to grab an imaginary ball from the air and mime the action of throwing this imaginary ball at the spectator's hand. Have him open his hand, revealing two balls.

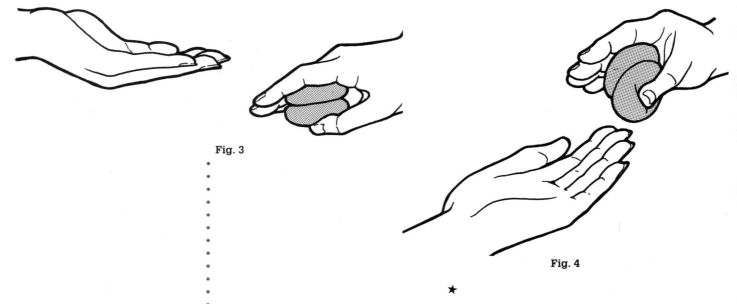

Fig. 3

Fig. 4

★

STEP 6: Place the two balls down on the table. With one of them execute the "Sponge-Ball Retention Vanish," but do not open your left hand. Now, pick up the other ball, adding the palmed one from the retention vanish. Place both of these balls, as one, into the spectator's hand and close his hand over them. Open your left hand, revealing that the ball has vanished, and have the spectator open his hand to reveal two balls.

★

STEP 7: Pick up one of the balls and do step 4 again. Place the ball you have taken from your pocket on the table. You will now have two balls lying on the table and one secretly palmed in your right hand.

Sequence C

STEP 8: You can now pick up one of the balls and add to it the ball you have palmed. Place these two, as one, into the spectator's hand. Pick up the third ball and execute the "Sponge-Ball Retention Vanish." Have him open his hand, revealing the ball.

★

STEP 9: With the palmed ball, execute steps 1 and 2, producing a third ball.

STEP 10: Now, execute the "Sponge-Ball Retention Vanish," but do not open your left hand. Instead, your left hand, still closed and presumably holding the ball, goes into your left pocket. There, it palms the ball already inside. Now, take the hand out, apparently leaving a ball inside. Your right hand now presses its secretly palmed ball against the outside of the left-hand pocket and then slowly pulls its fingers back, revealing the ball, making it appear as if it has penetrated through your pocket (figs. 5 and 6).

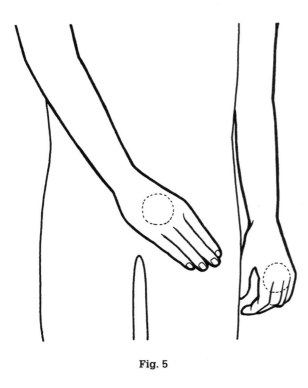

Fig. 5

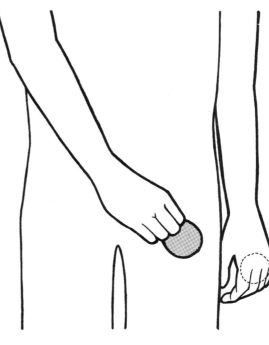

Fig. 6

★

STEP 11: Bring your left hand out from your pocket, palming the fourth ball that had been in the pocket.

Sequence D

STEP 12: With your left hand, pick up one of the balls from the table, adding it to the palmed ball. Hold the ball(s) in view as your right hand picks up a second ball from the table and places it in your left hand. Your left hand closes on all three balls, which will leave one remaining on the table. (The audience thinks there are only two in the left hand.) Your right hand places the remaining ball in your right pocket. The minute it is out of sight, open your left hand, revealing three balls. As the audience is looking at your left hand, your right hand comes out of your pocket with the fourth ball palmed.

★

STEP 13: Place the three balls from your left hand on the table. With your right hand, pick up one of them, adding it to the palmed ball as you did in step 5. Now, with your left hand, pick up one of the two remaining balls on the table. Place the two balls from your right hand (the audience believes there is only one) into your left hand, which closes over them along with the one ball already there. This will leave you with three balls in your left hand (the audience thinks there are only two) and one ball on the table. Pick up the remaining ball on the table with your right hand, and pretend to place it in your pocket, really palming it, as your right hand, and pretend to place it in your pocket, really palming it, as your right hand comes out of the pocket. Simultaneously, open your left hand to reveal all three balls. Once again, you have a ball palmed in your right hand and three balls on the table. Repeat the sequence above several times, fairly rapidly. By doing this, you will create a certain rhythm which will be necessary for the last step. On the last repetition, leave the fourth ball in your pocket, leaving only three balls in play.

★

STEP 14: This last step must be executed with the same rhythm as all of the repetitions. Pick up one of the balls with your right hand and execute the "Sponge-Ball Retention Vanish," but do not open your left hand. Take the other two balls and place them, along with the palmed ball, in your right pocket. Leave them all there. The audience will not notice that instead of two going in the hand and one in the pocket, you have apparently done the reverse—one in the hand, two in the pocket. In fact, there are none in the hand. The audience will think that this is another repetition of step 13. Pause to build suspense and suddenly clap your hands together, revealing the disappearance of all the balls.

Sponge-Ball Retention Vanish

STEP 1: Hold a sponge ball in your right hand, between your thumb and first two fingers (fig. 1). Extend your left palm a few inches below your right hand. Your right hand descends onto the palm of the left hand (fig. 2).

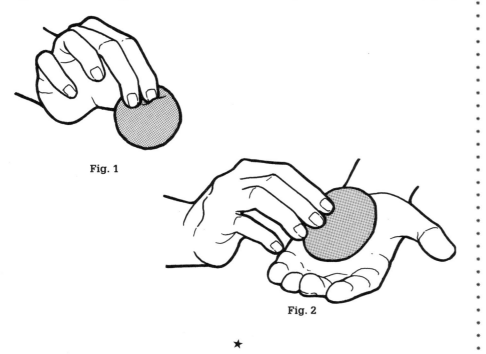

Fig. 1

Fig. 2

★

STEP 2: The fingers of your left hand begin to close. The move takes place when they completely hide the sponge ball from the audience's view (fig. 3).

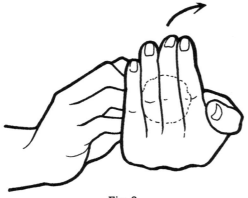

Fig. 3

Royal Magicians

Charles, Prince of Wales, heir apparent to England's throne, is a magician and a member of the venerable Magic Circle. This London club is a center of magic in Europe and throughout the world. He was inducted into membership after a masterful performance of the cups and balls, a classic of magic, first recorded on the walls of the Beni Hassan tomb in Egypt, in the twenty-fifth century B.C.

A generation earlier, his father, Prince Philip, the husband of Queen Elizabeth II, performed the time-honored "sawing a lady in half" before the selfsame Magic Circle.

Queen Elizabeth's late uncle Edward, Duke of Windsor, had for a time been King Edward VIII before abdicating the throne to marry Wallis Warfield Simpson, a divorced commoner from Blue Ridge Summit, Pennsylvania. While he was a resident of Buckingham Palace, King Edward would go backstage at the London theater where magician Howard Thurston was performing. There he would sit patiently on a prop trunk waiting for Thurston to finish his show, at which point the two men would exchange card tricks.

★

STEP 3: At this point, your right middle, ring, and pinkie fingers extend over the sponge ball (fig. 4). Once they are all the way over, they curl around the sponge ball as your forefinger releases its grip. Pull the ring and pinkie fingers in, finger palming the sponge ball. You will now move your right hand away as you close your left hand. When the time is right, open your left hand, revealing the sponge ball to be gone.

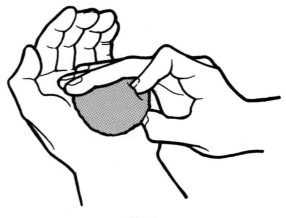

Fig. 4

Kitchen-Table Magic

itchen-table magic, magic with common objects, is often referred to as "impromptu magic." Magicians have not always had the luxury of credit card orders by phone. They were not always able to drive to the local magic shop and pick up the newest items. Until the early 1900s, magicians had either to make their own props or use objects found in the home.

The tricks in this section use such everyday objects as toothpicks, a drinking glass, and a book of matches. The special attraction of kitchen table magic is the contrast between these familiar objects and the startling effects they produce.

Magician Max Malini was performing before a group of congressmen and government officials in Washington, D.C. At a break in the performance, a distinguished senator snatched an orange from a bowl of fruit and tossed it to Malini, challenging him to change it to a lemon. The deed was done immediately. Then, Malini borrowed a $10 bill, made it disappear, and then reappear inside the lemon.

Jon Wooley, a computer software consultant, is an excellent restaurant magician. He loves to use the most common objects in his magic. For example, he waves a small tree branch rather than the usual finely crafted magic wand. Using the branch as a wand, he will tap the bottom of an inverted soup bowl, causing a fresh bagel to appear beneath.

The Electric Toothpicks

N O T E
★
This trick can also be done with wooden matches.

E F F E C T

Two toothpicks are shown. The magician claims that because wood is a poor conductor, the only type of electricity that can go through it is static electricity. The magician takes one toothpick and puts it on the edge of the table, leaving about half of it extending over the edge. He now takes the second toothpick and rubs it against his sleeve, claiming that it will generate electricity. He slowly takes this toothpick and carefully touches the toothpick that's hanging over the edge of the table. This toothpick jumps about a foot in the air, demonstrating the static electricity.

M E T H O D

STEP 1: You need two toothpicks for this trick. One of them is placed on the table so it hangs over the edge of the table (fig. 1).

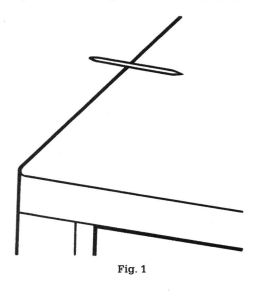

Fig. 1

★

STEP 2: Hold the second toothpick between your right thumb and index finger, with the middle finger on the underside of the toothpick. The toothpick should be gripped between your middle finger's fingertip and its nail, and the middle finger should push upward. This will put pressure on the toothpick (figs. 2 and 3).

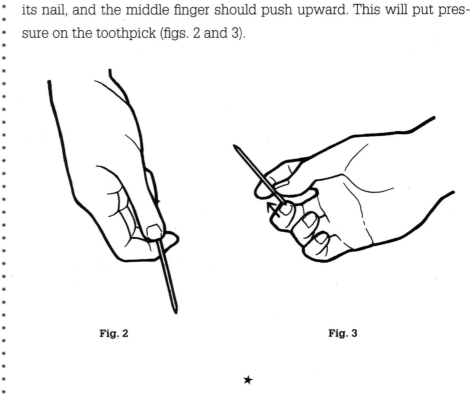

Fig. 2   **Fig. 3**

★

STEP 3: Discuss static electricity and carry on other patter. When you're ready, rub the toothpick on your sleeve, saying that this will generate static electricity. Slowly bring the toothpick to the position depicted in fig. 4.

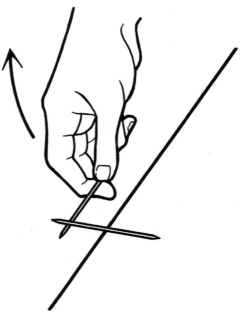

Fig. 4

★

STEP 4: Raise the toothpick held by your right hand up toward the tabled toothpick. When they touch, your middle fingernail flicks the end of the toothpick, which is firmly held in place by your thumb and forefinger (this motion is minuscule and invisible to the audience). This will snap the held toothpick against the tabled toothpick, causing it to jump into the air (fig. 5).

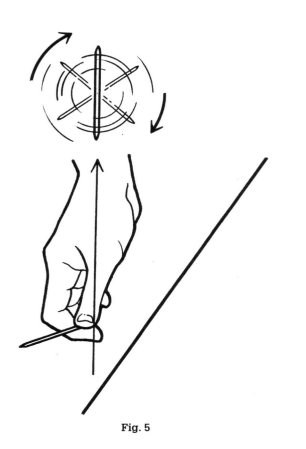

Fig. 5

Another neat application of the "flicking" move used in this routine involves a wooden match. Light the match and let it burn until less than an inch is left. Now, blow it out carefully, making sure the carbonized wood doesn't break. Pretend to pluck a hair off of someone's head, and pantomime as if you're wrapping it around the head of the match. Now, with a jerk of the imaginary hair, used simultaneously with the flicking move (which will send the match head flying), it will appear as if you have, with an imaginary hair, taken the head right off the match.

N O T E

★

Until you are confident you can handle this trick flawlessly, I would advise against using fine crystal.

The Glass Through Table

EFFECT

The magician shows a coin, a sturdy drinking glass, and a sheet of newspaper, folded in quarters. He explains that a glass such as this, with a thick base, has the ability to serve as a sort of hammer. He says that you can hit an object very hard with the glass and the glass won't break as long as you hit it the right way. He begins to demonstrate by holding the glass at the top and hammering (gently) on the coin with the edge of the base of the glass. The magician places the glass on top of the coin. Next, he wraps the newspaper over and around the glass, "just in case the glass shatters."

The magician displays the coin one last time and sets the glass flat on top of the coin. He then says that hitting the coin with the glass hard enough will drive the coin right through the table. He counts one . . . two . . . THREE! and slams his hand down on the glass. The paper covering is flattened and the glass disappears but is quickly revealed by the magician removing it from under the table with his other hand. The glass, not the coin, penetrated right through the tabletop. Finally, the newspaper is lifted, showing that the coin is in exactly the same place as it was in the beginning of the trick.

METHOD

STEP 1: You must be sitting at a table. Have a heavy glass with a thick base and a sheet of newspaper. Borrow a coin and explain how, if hit correctly, the glass can drive the coin right through the table. Put the glass on top of the coin and wrap the newspaper over the glass, as shown in fig. 1.

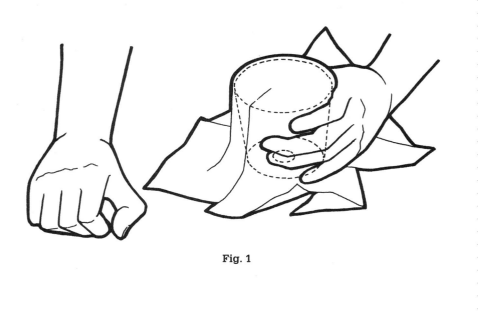

Fig. 1

★

STEP 2: Holding the glass with your right hand, tap the bottom edge against the coin a few times. Now lift up the glass, newspaper and all, revealing the coin, supposedly to check its position. Bring the glass with newspaper back to the table edge, over your lap, as shown in fig. 2. Do this as you explain that a glass with a thick enough base can drive the

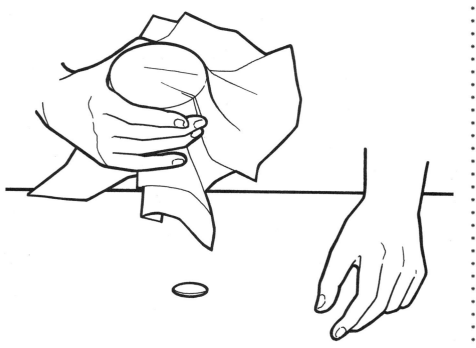

Fig. 2

coin through the table. Still talking, drop the glass into your lap (fig. 3). Good misdirection for this secret action would be to gesture, with the left hand, to the coin that lays on the table. Hold the newspaper shell lightly so as not to crush it. Bring the newspaper shell back over the coin, but because the newspaper shell is intact, it will look as if the glass is still there.

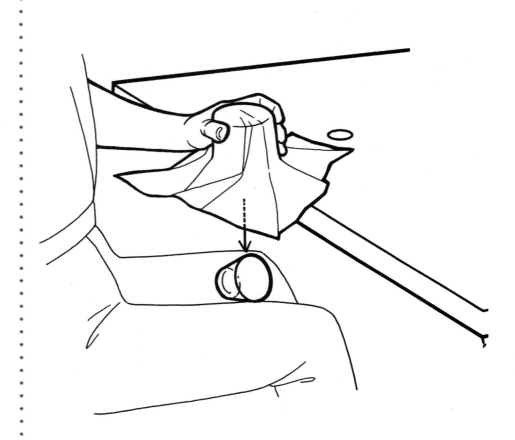

Fig. 3

★

STEP 3: For the deception to work, you must handle the newspaper shell as if there really were a glass there. Put the newspaper in the shape of the glass back over the coin. Continue to hold it with one of your hands, making sure it doesn't fall over or lose its shape.

★

STEP 4: Explain that on the count of three, you will use the glass to drive the coin through the table. One . . . two . . . THREE! Smash your hand down on the "glass" (fig. 4) and it will look as if it goes right through the table. Reach under with your free hand, grab the glass from your lap, and move it further away from you under the table before pulling it out for all to see. Now lift up the newspaper, revealing the coin still there.

C O M M E N T

★

This same trick can be done with a salt shaker rather than a glass.

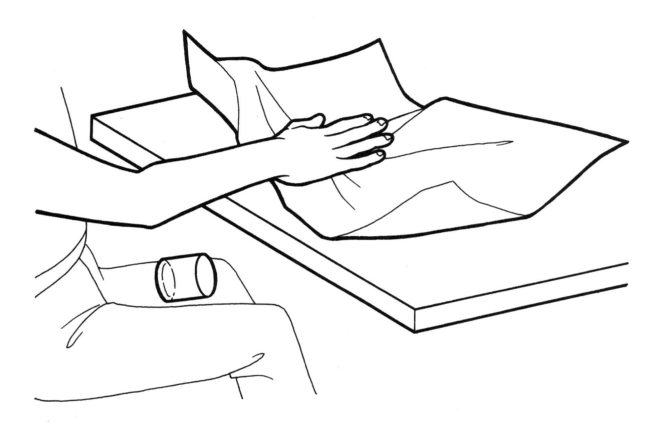

Fig. 4

The Missing Match

E F F E C T

A matchbook is shown and opened. The magician rips out one of the matches, lights it, and quickly blows it out. The match then vanishes. The matchbook is opened, and it is found that the burned-out match has returned, reappearing in the place from which it was originally removed.

P R E P A R A T I O N

You must have a relatively complete matchbook. If you are at a restaurant, excuse yourself, get a book of the restaurant's matches, and secretly alter the matchbook as follows: First, take out one match from the matchbook. Then, take a second match from the center of the first row of matches, carefully fold forward and straight down, and close the flap (fig. 1). MAKE SURE THE FLAP IS CLOSED!!! With the matchbook closed, light the removed match, and use it to light the match that is sticking out from the book (fig. 2). Now, quickly blow both matches out. Throw away the one that is not in the book. Let the match still in the book cool, open the flap, put the match back where it was, and close the flap. You are all set to go.

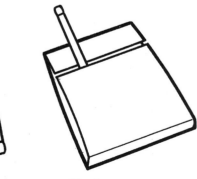

Fig. 1

M E T H O D

STEP 1: Open the matchbook so that the matches are facing you.

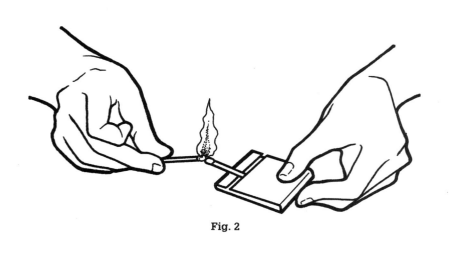

Fig. 2

★

STEP 2: Move your left thumb onto the head of the burned match. You will now move the matchbook downward so the audience can see the matches. As you do this, your thumb simply folds the match over so that it is concealed (fig. 3).

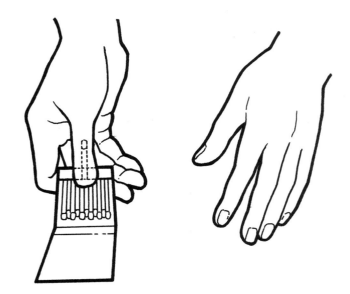

Fig. 3

★

STEP 3: Now, rip out the match next to the concealed match.

STEP 4: You are now going to close the matchbook. Bring your right-hand fingers up under the back of the cover and fold it up toward you. As you do this, under the cover of your right hand, simply flip the burnt out match back into its original position with your left thumb. Continue closing the matchbook cover with your right hand until it is completely closed, using the left thumb if necessary to accomplish the task. To continue, rotate the matchbook over to expose the striking surface.

★

STEP 5: Now, strike the ripped-out match with your right hand. Quickly shake it to extinguish it. Put the matchbook down on the table with your left hand. Continue to shake the match. Ask a spectator to hold out his hand. As he is doing this, in the motion of shaking the match, just throw it over your shoulder (fig. 4). Continue to shake as if cooling down the match. Now, slowly bring your right hand toward the spectator's hand and show your hand empty.

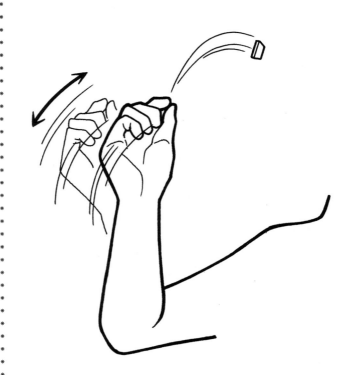

Fig. 4

STEP 6: Wave your hand over the matchbook and have someone else open it. (This way the audience *knows* there is no trickery involved.) They will see the match back in what they will think was its original position and be terribly impressed.

No Dice

EFFECT

The magician shows a die, one of a pair of dice, to have a six on one side and a one on the other. The die is tapped on the table, and it is now shown to have a five opposite the six. A spectator taps the die on the table, turns it over, and the die has returned to its original state: six on one side, one on the other.

METHOD

STEP 1: The die lies on the table. Pick it up between the tips of your right index finger and thumb. Fix it so that a six is on top, a one is on the bottom, and your index finger is against the five (fig. 1).

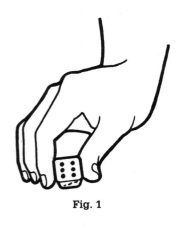

Fig. 1

★

STEP 2: Turn your hand palm up, showing a one opposite the six (fig. 2). Turn your hand back over.

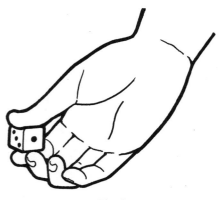

Fig. 2

★

STEP 3: Tap the die on the table. Now you are going to do the following move to show that a five is on the opposite side of the six. The move duplicates the movement in step 2, but your index finger pulls down on the die and your thumb pushes up, rotating the die between the two fingers (figs. 3 and 4). When your hand is palm up, the audience will see a five on the opposite side of the six.

For this trick, a smaller die is easier to manipulate. Casino dice will not work for two reasons. The first is that they are clear, and the second is that their edges are not rounded at all, making the move harder.

Fig. 3

Fig. 4

★

STEP 4: To turn it back over, just bring your fingers back to their original position by doing the same movement in reverse.

★

STEP 5: Now place the die on the table, six side up. Ask the spectator to tap it on the table and turn it over, revealing a one on the opposite side of the six once again.

Conjuring with Clairvoyance

Jean Eugene Robert-Houdin, known as "The Father of Modern Magic," performed a mind-reading act, "Second Sight," with his son Emile. Emile, blindfolded, would correctly identify items his father borrowed from spectators, the colors of hidden objects, and various drinks tasted by audience members.

This act, mentalism from a distance, or "remote viewing," became popular in the twentieth century. In the 1920s, mentalist/magician Theodore Anneman and his wife, Greta, performed the act that Robert-Houdin originated seventy-five years before, calling it "En Rapport." Annemann, a severely troubled man, took his life at the age of thirty-four. During his brief career, however, he gained a reputation, which lasts to this day within the magic community, as one of the greatest mentalists of all time.

Related to acts in which a blindfolded performer correctly answers questions normally requiring sight is an act involving a disembodied, "talking head." Psychologist and great coin-magician Dr. Sol Stone first got interested in magic as a young boy, when he was taken to a Howard Thurston magic show. In the hallway of the theater, as an attraction, was a woman's head resting on a sword. The head would answer questions from passersby. What did Master Stone ask her? "How do you go to the bathroom?" Though the head declined to answer, Stone was hooked.

The escape artist Harry Houdini made a feature of naming people in the town where he was performing who had recently died. How did he do it? In advance of his performance, he delved into the local newspaper's obituary notices and took a quick stroll through the town's cemetery. However, Houdini's purpose was not to entertain—it was to demonstrate that spiritualism was a fraud.

Joseph Dunninger, perhaps the most famous mentalist of all time, performed incredible mental effects over radio and on national television. Dunninger would read the thoughts of a skydiver in flight above the studio or "see" the serial numbers on new $20 bills that were being held inside a bank vault. He even predicted a word that New York mayor Jimmy Walker would choose at random.

Dunninger was called a fake, however, by magician and orchestra leader Richard Himber. Himber claimed that there was no way that Dunninger could actually read minds, particularly his. Dunninger's response to Mr. Himber: "First Himber has to prove to me he has a mind to read." Another's of Dunninger's favorite responses to skeptics was, "To those who don't believe, no explanation is possible. For those that do, no explanation is necessary."

Newspaper Prediction

EFFECT

The magician calls up two spectators. One of them is asked to be the guardian of a sealed envelope, which he is given. The other is shown a folded newspaper. He is instructed to place this newspaper behind his back and unfold it there so no one can see a single word on the front page. Therefore, the magician explains, the choice the spectator is about to make will be completely uninfluenced. The spectator follows these instructions. He is then handed a marker, and with the newspaper still behind his back, he is instructed to make a circle of about two inches in diameter anywhere on the page. The spectator does this and is then asked to bring forward the marker and the newspaper. The circled sentences are read, the envelope is opened, and the piece of paper that was inside the envelope is shown to have accurately predicted the exact sentences circled by the spectator.

PREPARATION

Quite a bit of setup is required for this incredible trick. The materials used are commonly found around the house. However, this is not a trick you will be able to do in impromptu circumstances. It is a trick designed for a more formal show.

You will need two matching markers for this trick. One of them must be left without its caps for however long it takes for it to dry out *completely.* When it is finally dried out, put the cap back on. Now obtain a copy of the day's newspaper. With the working marker, make a circle on the front page, about two inches in diameter, around a piece of text. Type on a piece of paper the sentences in that text. Put the typed paper in a sealed envelope. Fold over the newspaper so the front page in unseen, and you are all set.

METHOD

STEP 1: Take out the folded newspaper, the dry marker, and the envelope. Invite two spectators to assist you and give one of them the envelope. Explain to the other that he is to place the newspaper behind his back,

N O T E
★

My preference is to use a newspaper in this trick, but a book or a magazine can be used as well.

The late, great mentalist Dr. Stanley Jaks was famous for predicting weeks ahead of time a story that would appear in the newspaper. One of his performances was before an audience of newspapermen in Bern, Switzerland. He had sent them a prediction of a headline, in a sealed envelope, three weeks before the performance. Finally, the envelope was slit open and the prediction revealed. The headline read: JEALOUS HUSBAND MURDERS WIFE IN RAGE. Jaks's prediction was correct—the headline appeared on that day's newspaper. The next day, Jaks found himself at police headquarters, being questioned about the murder by three suspicious detectives.

This trick lends itself to dramatic enhancement. Let's say you have a business meeting the next day and want to open with some magic. Send a letter, via next day mail, to a person who will be attending the meeting. Within the mailing envelope, include a smaller, sealed envelope that contains your prediction. In your cover note, ask your colleague to bring the smaller envelope, still sealed, to the meeting. At the meeting, make a big thing of announcing that the prediction envelope arrived earlier that day. When it is finally opened, the reaction will be much stronger than if you had just brought it with you yourself.

unfold it, and draw a small circle somewhere on the front page, about two inches in diameter. Give him the newspaper and the uncapped marker and make sure he does as instructed.

★

STEP 2: Of course, the marker will not draw, but he does not know this. Have him bring out the newspaper and have him read the words he circled.

★

STEP 3: Now ask the other spectator to rip open the envelope and read the words written on the paper . . . an exact match.

Annual Prediction

EFFECT

The magician hands a spectator an envelope with a prediction inside. The magician then asks to borrow a quarter from another spectator. The magician then hands this quarter to the spectator holding the prediction. This spectator is asked to read off the year that is on the quarter. The envelope is ripped open, and the prediction inside is the exact same year as the quarter.

METHOD

STEP 1: This little mental miracle can be done anywhere. The setup is as follows: You need to look at a quarter and remember the year. Place this quarter in your right pocket. On a piece of paper, write the year that was on the quarter and put the paper in an envelope and seal it. When you're ready to go, hand the envelope to someone, and classic palm the quarter in the right hand. (See "Palming" on page 108.)

★

STEP 2: Borrow a quarter from someone. Take it in your left hand and execute the "Shuttle Pass" (page 110). In a flowing motion, hand the previously palmed quarter to the spectator who is holding the prediction. Have him read the year on the quarter. Have him rip open the prediction to find that it is accurate.

COMMENTS
★

Obviously, this is a very simple trick in its method. The impact of this trick depends on the buildup you give it. Be careful that the quarter whose year you have memorized is not too shiny or too dark so the borrowed quarter won't look radically different.

Pulse Reading

EFFECT

A card is selected by the spectator and replaced in the deck. The deck is spread, face up, on the table. The spectator then closes his hand into a fist and extends his index finger. The magician grips the spectator's wrist. He says that he is going to wave the spectator's hand over the deck and attempt to find the card. He explains that the spectator's pulse rate will rise when the finger passes over the selected card. The spectator's finger is waved over the deck, and the magician removes a large portion of the deck, saying that he now has a sense for the general area of where the card is located. This is done once more, leaving only three cards on the table. One last time, and two of the three are eliminated. The last card is the card previously selected by the spectator.

METHOD

Step 1: Execute the "Hindu-Shuffle Force" as described in "Card Magic" on page 67. Now, you can hand the deck to the spectator for shuffling. He can shuffle all he wants because you know what his card is.

★

STEP 2: Execute the face-up "Ribbon Spread," as described in "Card Magic" on page 53. Have the spectator extend his index finger and grip his wrist. Slowly, wave his hand over the deck (fig. 1). While you are do-

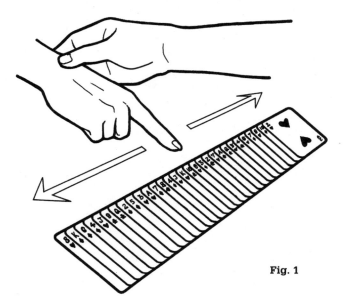

Fig. 1

ing this, locate the forced card. When you have found it, state that you have located the general area in which you believe the card will be found. Eliminate all of the cards except for six, one of them being the forced card. The card should be the fifth card in from the end (fig. 2).

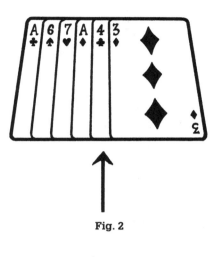

Fig. 2

★

STEP 3: Wave the spectator's wrist again, and eliminate the first three cards, saying you're sure it's not one of them.

★

STEP 4: Spread out the three remaining cards so that they are separated. Slowly touch the spectator's index finger to each card. Slide forward the forced card with the spectator's finger, revealing the selected card.

N O T E

★

This effect can be performed just about anywhere. All you need are three small sheets of paper, a pen, an opaque drinking glass, and a spectator.

Triple Play

EFFECT

The magician tells the spectator that he is going to perform an act of telepathy. The magician takes a pen and paper and writes down a prediction. He folds the paper over, labels it "change," and drops it into a glass. The magician then asks the spectator to reach into his pocket and pull out all the change he has in his pocket and to count it. The spectator is asked to remember that amount. The magician writes a second prediction, folds the paper over, and labels it "name." It, too, is dropped into the glass. The spectator is then asked to call out the name of a close friend. The magician writes a third prediction and labels it "flower." It is dropped into the glass, and the spectator is asked to call out a type of flower. The predictions are dumped out of the glass, read, and are all shown to be correct.

METHOD

STEP 1: For this you will need three pieces of paper and a pen. Pick up the first piece of paper and write on the inside, without letting anyone see, ROSE. Fold the paper over. Now say that you will label this prediction CHANGE. Instead, on the front of it, without letting anyone see, write, FLOWER. The audience should have no reason to suspect that you are deceiving them at this point. Drop this prediction into the glass.

★

STEP 2: Have the spectator take out the change that he has in his pocket, and have him count it. Instruct him to remember this amount. You should remember it also.

★

STEP 3: Take the next piece of paper and write on it the amount of change that was just displayed. Do not let anyone see this. Now, fold the paper over and, hidden, write CHANGE. on the front, while claiming that you are labeling it NAME. This labeling deception, in all cases, should be done nonchalantly. Even though the audience doesn't see what you're writing, they should have no reason to suspect you are lying about the label.

★

STEP 4: Have the spectator call out a first name. It can be of a friend, relative, or whatever. Nod your head to indicate you heard the name. Repeat the name to ensure the spectator remembers that this was the name he selected.

★

STEP 5: Pick up the last piece of paper and write on it the name that was just called. Let no one see what you have written. Fold the paper over and label it NAME, under the pretense of labeling it FLOWER.

★

STEP 6: Now, instruct the spectator to name "the first type of flower that pops into your mind." On this one, you have to sort of rush them. Most of the time, they will say "rose." If you are worried about this not working, see *Comments* for other thoughts on this subject.

★

STEP 7: Have them pour out the contents of the glass, open up the predictions, and they will see that they are all correct.

COMMENTS
★

As for people not saying "rose," it will happen. When I perform this trick, if the person does not say "rose," I have them pour out the contents and show that I got two out of three right. However, if you want to make this trick foolproof, instead of using a flower, force a card. Use the "Hindu-Shuffle Force," as described on page 67. Therefore you can, if you wish, simply replace ROSE with the name of the forced card, and FLOWER with CARD. It is now a foolproof trick.

As for the labeling, do not be overly cautious. The audience should have no reason to suspect that you are dissembling about the labeling. However, if you go to great lengths to hide the label they *will* suspect. Just treat it casually.

Magic Influentials

*I*n the history of every business, hobby, profession, or art form, including magic, there are people whose contributions, though of lasting importance, may not be evident. In the modern history of magic, especially in the latter half of the twentieth century, there have been many such magicians. A few of these special people come to mind.

The late Louis Tannen was the founder, in 1939, and longtime genial proprietor of Louis Tannen, Inc., a New York City magic shop, and publisher of many magic books. Tannen's was, and remains today under the ownership of John Blake and Tony Spina, a center of magic in New York City and throughout the world.

Leonard Greenfader, a crusty former motorcycle policeman, has for more than twenty years been the membership chairman of both Assembly #1, known as the "Parent Assembly," of the Society of American Magicians, and separately, of Ring #26 of the International Brotherhood of Magicians. The two clubs, both based in New York, are the largest in their respective organizations and include such well-known magicians as David Copperfield and

Phone-Book Mystery

EFFECT

A phone book and a deck of cards lie on the table. The magician picks up the deck and runs cards, face down, through his hands and asks the spectator to say "stop!" anywhere. At that point, the next three cards are said to represent a page in the phone book. The fourth card represents a line number. The magician is not allowed to see the cards. The phone book is opened to the page determined by the cards. The lines are then counted down to the appropriate line number. The magician correctly calls off the name, address, and phone number of the line that was selected.

PREPARATION

For this trick, you need to have mastered the "Hindu-Shuffle Force" as described in "Card Magic" on page 67. A little bit of memorization is required for this trick. You need to select one page in a White Pages book, a three-digit page. Let's assume this is page 235. Now count down to the, let's say, seventh line. Memorize the name, address, and phone number on the first column of line 7 on page 235. Now, put in order, at the face of the deck, a two, a three, a five, and a seven (fig. 1). Put the deck in its case, and you are all set to go.

Fig. 1

★

STEP 1: Execute the "Hindu-Shuffle Force." When the spectator stops you, have him take the bottom three cards off, together, to represent the page number (fig. 2). Then have him remember the next card to represent the line number.

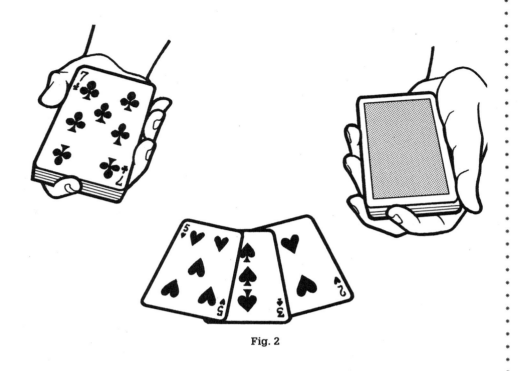

Fig. 2

★

STEP 2: Have him open the book to that page and look at that line. Now, a little bit of acting, and then tell him what you memorized earlier.

Harry Blackstone, Jr. Greenfader, a skilled close-up magician and much sought after master of ceremonies, is considered by many to be the unofficial mayor of the New York magic community.

If there is a first family in the modern world of magic, arguably it would be the Larsens. William W. Larsen, Sr., who died in 1953 at the age of forty-eight, was founder of *Genii* magazine, established in 1936, now the oldest independent U.S. magic magazine in continuous existence. His son, William, Jr., took over the helm after his father's death. He and his brother Milt, in 1963, converted a marvelous old Hollywood mansion into the Magic Castle, a dream of their father's, a place where the art of magic would be performed and enjoyed. The Magic Castle is a multistage performance center, restaurant, and club. Many working magicians owe their successes to the first break given to them and the continued interest shown in their careers by the Magic Castle, under the Larsen brothers. Erika Larsen, granddaughter of *Genii's* founder, took over as editor of *Genii* after her father's death in 1993.

Rope Magic

ew tricks are more famous than the Indian rope trick, in which a boy climbs a rope that mysteriously rises from the ground and becomes rigid. Reports of this trick go as far back as the eighth century, when the theologian and author Shankara discussed it in his book, *The Crest Jewel of Discrimination*. Shankara believed no trickery was involved, and the rope was manipulated by an unseen, mystical force. But modern magicians and other investigators, despite sustained efforts and the offer of large rewards, have never been able to find a street performer, or *jadoo wallah*, who could perform it as described. Modern magicians' versions of the rising rope have been performed by such magicians as Harry Blackstone, Sr., Howard Thurston, and Doug Henning. Currently, in India, jadoo wallah still perform versions of the trick where the rope rises and becomes rigid, but no one attempts to climb it.

College Kids Eating Goldfish

The late Chicago magician Matt Schulien owned a restaurant called Schulien's, which still thrives today. At the restaurant, he loved to perform an effect in which he reached, with a carrot sliver palmed in his hand, into a fishbowl filled with goldfish. He'd pull his hand out, holding the carrot sliver, which he would then immediately eat. Schulien had actually perfected a way of shaking the carrot piece to make it look, momentarily, like a goldfish. Legend has it that one night a group of college students watched Schulien do this. They were so convinced Schulien had actually eaten a goldfish that they went back to their campus and tried it themselves. The 1920s craze of college kids eating goldfish had been born!

Dr. Sol Stone

*D*r. Sol Stone, psychologist and magician, was a navigator for the United States Army Air Force in World War II. On his twenty-sixth bombing mission, his plane was shot down over Hungary. He and the rest of the crew survived the crash and ran for cover. A Russian infantry patrol found them. For the next thirty-eight days, Dr. Stone performed magic for the Russian troops, liberated prisoners of war, and people freed from death camps. Dr. Stone recalls, "If you could arouse their sense of wonder and delight, even if for only a few minutes, for those few minutes it gave them relief from the stress and strain of the war."

Rope magic had its beginnings in false spiritualism. A bound medium's secret escape provided the first deceptions with rope. Chippewa Indians, living in the upper Midwest, in the 1780s performed sacred rituals inside tents that shook with spirits, despite the fact that the medicine man inside was securely tied with rope. This feat is replicated by magicians today, including David Copperfield. It is called the "Spirit Cabinet."

The pioneer of modern rope magic, Milbourne Christopher, created the effect of stretching a rope from a few inches to a few yards. The rope was then examined and found not to be stretchable. At the age of twenty-one, he showed this trick to President Franklin Roosevelt and his wife in 1935 at the Roosevelts' White House Easter Monday party. Christopher could cause ropes to knot at his command, magically untie them, and cut and restore them. For *Look* magazine photographers he had a girl climb a rope that had risen into the air. An ashtray in his house was even held up by a rigid rope ascending from the ground.

Rope magic appeals to both magicians and their audiences because rope is a simple prop and because the magical effects involving rope are easy for an audience to follow.

Ring and Rope

N O T E

★

For this trick, you will need a piece of rope about four feet long and a ring about three or four inches in diameter. A ladies' bracelet would do just fine, although I use a heavy brass ring specifically designed for this trick.

E F F E C T

A magician hands out a ring and a rope for examination. They are handed back, and the magician threads the ring onto the rope. Moments later, the ring seems to melt right through the rope.

M E T H O D

STEP 1: Hand the ring and the rope out for examination.

★

STEP 2: Thread the ring onto the rope and hold the rope by its ends with your right hand. Hold the rope so the ring opening faces the audience. Note that one strand is on the audience side, or front of the ring, and the other strand is on the magician's side, or back of the ring. The move you are about to make is going to be covered by what you say, so follow these next three steps precisely.

★

STEP 3: You ask, "Did you examine the rope?" They audience will say, "Yes." Then say, "And there are no holes or trap doors in it?" As you say this, your left hand grasps the rope just below the halfway mark (fig. 1).

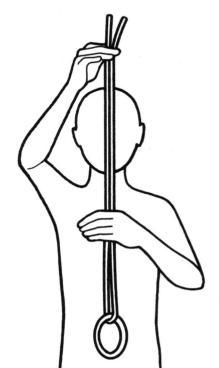

Fig. 1

★

STEP 4: Now let go of the ends with your right hand. Let the front half, or audience strand, of the rope fall in front of your hand and in front of the ring and the back half, or magician's strand, fall over your thumb and behind the ring (fig. 2). As this is happening, the audience will say, "None." This entire sequence only takes a second.

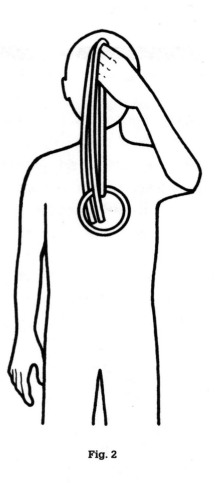

Fig. 2

★

STEP 5: Now, you say, "And did you examine the ring?" Yes. "And there are no holes in this either?" None. Now, here's the move. Your right hand grasps the back half of rope, which should be on the side of the ring facing you, moves through the ring, and grasps the front end of the rope (fig. 3). Your right hand now pulls both ends through the ring and back to your side (fig. 4). This takes place as you make the gag, in response to the no holes statement, "Except for this one here in the center. Hee, hee, hah, hah."

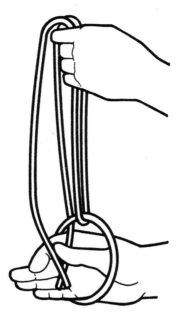

Fig. 3

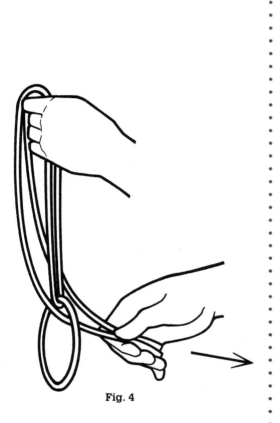

Fig. 4

★

STEP 6: Pull the ends of the rope straight down with your right hand, raising the ring up into your waiting left hand. Your left hand now closes into a fist over the rope and the now dislodged ring. The patter I use here is "This is what's known as the elevator ring." At this point your left hand lets go of the center of the rope, letting it fall free. I add, "But sometimes the cable breaks." You can hand out the ring and the rope for examination once again.

Rope Through Neck

E F F E C T

A magician takes a rope and twists it around his neck twice. He then holds the two ends and pulls the rope through his neck.

CAUTION: As you are first learning and practicing this trick, when you come to step 4, pull VERY SLOWLY. Continue to do it slowly, until you have the trick down pat.

M E T H O D

STEP 1: Hang a length of rope about six feet long around your neck. Make sure it hangs lower on the left side (fig. 1). With your right hand, reach across and grab the left-hand rope (fig. 2).

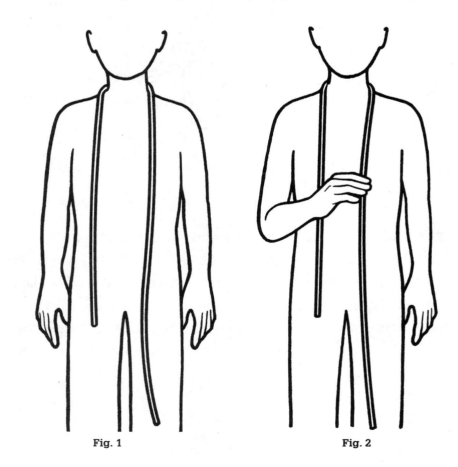

Fig. 1   Fig. 2

STEP 2: With your right hand, pull the piece of rope, holding it where depicted in fig. 2, to the right and up (fig. 3), and halfway around your neck.
(Fig. 4 is from the back.) Make sure the hanging end of the piece of rope
in your right hand is to the LEFT; adjust it with your left hand, if necessary

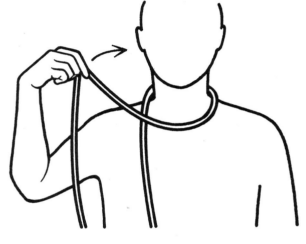

Fig. 3

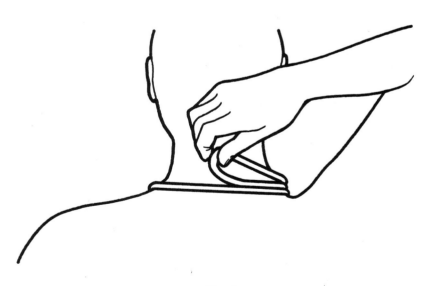

Fig. 4

(fig. 5 shows it from the front; if it is to the right, you will end up *actually* wrapping the rope around your neck). Now, bring your left hand back around the left side of your neck. There, transfer the loop that the right hand is holding to the left hand's grasp, held in place by the index finger (figs. 6 and 7). Now, bring your right hand back down and grasp the piece of rope on the right.

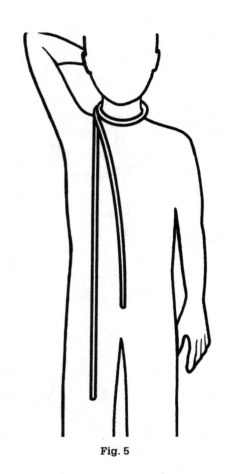

Fig. 5

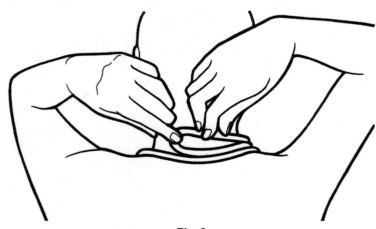

Fig. 6

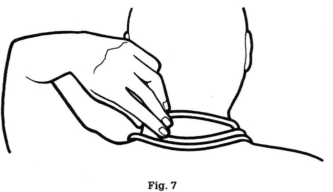

Fig. 7

★

STEP 3: Pull this piece to the right and up, and then all the way around your neck, over the index finger, and onto your chest (fig. 8). Do not let go of the piece of rope held by your right hand. Behind your neck, your left thumb pinches the loop against your left index finger. In a small motion, move the loop to the left and then to the right while your right hand

Fig. 8

keeps taut the hanging end it is holding. The friction between the loops of rope at the back of your neck will hold the rope in place around your neck after you remove your hand. Go for it; drop your left hand (figs. 9 and 10).

★

STEP 4: Now, with your two hands, grasp the two hanging ends and pull! Voilà, the rope penetrates your neck.

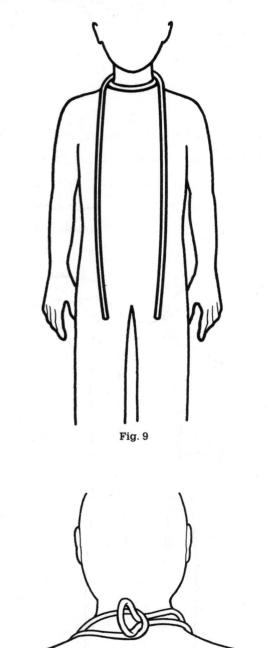

Fig. 9

Fig. 10

Cut and Restored Rope

N O T E
★

Magician Jeff Sheridan performed regularly in New York's Central Park between 1968 and 1982. He has restored thousands of ropes, entertaining thousands of people, including the late John Lennon, a member of the Beatles, undoubtedly the most influential group in rock music history. After one performance, Lennon said to Sheridan, "Many would like the Beatles to rejoin as easily as those ropes of yours. You're the best magician I have ever seen."

EFFECT

The magician displays a piece of rope and a pair of scissors. He cuts the rope in the exact center, yet when the two pieces are displayed, one is longer than the other. He trims the longer rope to make it even, yet the ropes remain unequal. The magician ties the ends of the two ropes together and winds the rope around his fist. He waves his hand over his fist, and when the rope is unraveled, the knot has disappeared and the two pieces of rope have been restored.

METHOD

STEP 1: For this trick, you will need a six-foot length of rope and a pair of very sharp scissors. If you wish, you can run a length of clothesline through your washing machine to make it softer and more pliable. Magic stores sell scissors specifically designed for rope cutting, but you needn't buy these. Just make sure the scissors you decide to use can easily cut through the rope. Okay, on to the trick. Hold the rope in your left hand, as depicted in fig. 1.

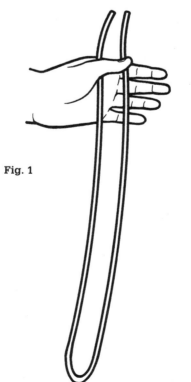

Fig. 1

★

STEP 2: Bring up the center of the rope to the position depicted in fig. 2, holding it between your right thumb and fingers. Now, as part of the same motion, your right fingers reach through the looped center and grab the piece of rope on the right (fig. 3). Pull this loop up and above your hand, clipping it against your left fingers with your left thumb, and move your right hand away. This will leave you in a position depicted in figs. 4 and 5 (4 is your view, 5 is the audience's).

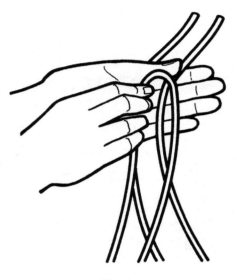

Fig. 2

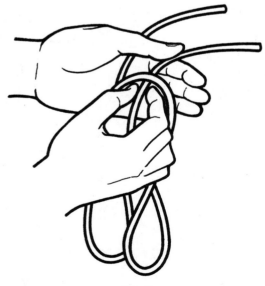

Fig. 3

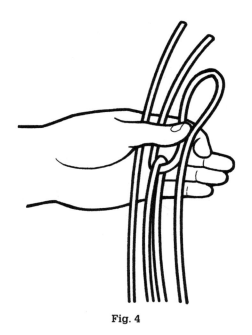

Fig. 4

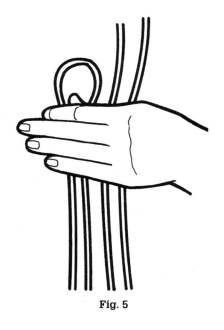

Fig. 5

★

STEP 3: If step 2 was done in a flowing motion, the audience will believe that the loop exposed above your left hand is at the exact center of the rope. Pick up the scissors with your free hand and cut the loop. For the purposes of these instructions, we will now label the ends, from left to right, 1, 2, 3, and 4, respectively (fig. 6). You now hold on to ends 2 and 3, but let 1 and 4 fall. It will appear as if you are holding the two pieces of rope, but really a small piece is interlocked with a long piece. (Fig. 7 is the audience's view, fig. 8 is your view.) However, as the audience sees it, one of the pieces of rope appears to be about five inches longer than the other (fig. 8, again).

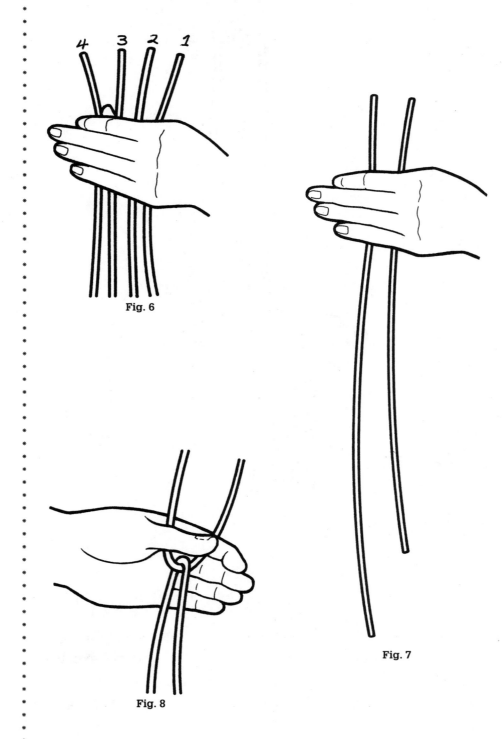

Fig. 6

Fig. 7

Fig. 8

STEP 4: Comment on the difference in length between the two pieces of rope. Cut the extra length from the longer rope, to even out the two pieces (fig. 9). As you cut, pull downward with the scissors. This way, even after you cut the longer rope, apparently making the two pieces equal in length, they are still uneven. This is not only magical but also pretty funny. You will be back to the position depicted in fig. 7.

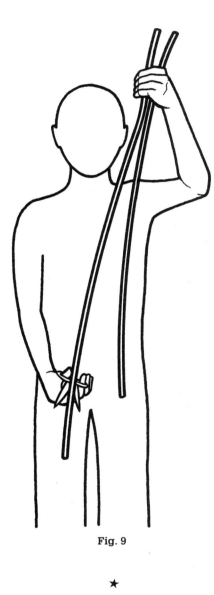

Fig. 9

★

STEP 5: Now you will have two ends sticking out above your hand. Tie them together in a conventional, single knot. The audience will believe that you have tied the two pieces of rope together, but in reality, you have just tied the little piece *around* the larger piece.

★

STEP 6: Now grip one of the ends of the rope with the left hand. Grab the rope, right where the knot is, with your right hand. Begin to wrap the rope around your left hand (fig. 10). When you get to the point where the part of the rope with the knot on it is about to be wrapped around the hand, just hold onto the knot with your right hand. It will slide down the rope, and, if you continue wrapping the rope *all* the way around, the knot will come off the rope (fig. 11).

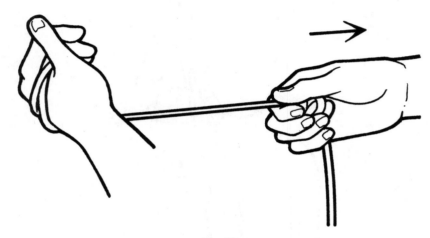

Fig. 10

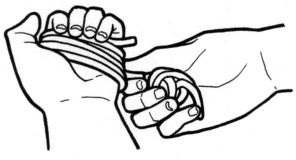

Fig. 11

★

STEP 7: Quickly move your right hand toward the scissors and pick them up, continuing to palm the knot. The scissors will hide the unnatural position that your right hand is in because of the palmed knot. Wave the scissors over the left hand. The scissors are, in the spectator's mind, being used as sort of a transmitter of magic.

★

STEP 8: Now, place the scissors in your right pocket. While you are there, simply drop the palmed knot. Unwrap the rope, displaying it whole.

N O T E

★

This trick has been around since the pharaohs. However, the modern method of performing "Professor's Nightmare" has been credited to Bob Carver. Today, it is often used by Project Magic, a network of magicians founded by David Copperfield. This organization helps occupational therapists working to rehabilitate patients with damaged motor skills by teaching them simple sleight of hand.

Lawyer Peter Kougasian does a fantastic rope routine and says that among his favorite magicians, most are those who perform the classics. "It doesn't necessarily have to be a new trick or an ingenious new method to be magical." This trick certainly fits the bill.

Steven Okulewicz uses this routine in his geology lectures. He uses the ropes to represent chemical bonds and shows how they can be stretched.

Professor's Nightmare

E F F E C T

A magician displays three pieces of rope—one is very short, the next is medium length, and the last is long. Then, all of a sudden, the ropes are shown to be of equal length. The magician ties these equal sized ropes together, leaving the magician with one, knotted, HUGE piece of rope. He then wraps this rope around his fist. When it is unwrapped, it is shown that the knots have moved and the ropes restored to their original lengths. The ropes are untied, displayed, and thrown to the audience, to be kept by whoever catches them.

M E T H O D

STEP 1: For this trick, you will need three lengths of rope: one is ten inches long, a second is twenty-three inches, and the third is thirty-six inches. Have them examined. Now, retrieve from the audience the longest length of rope and hold it, near one of its ends, in your left hand. Hold it against your hand with your thumb (fig. 1).

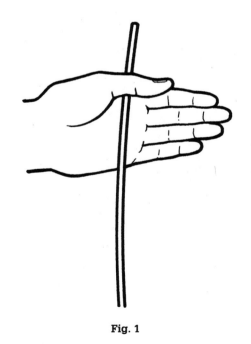

Fig. 1

★

STEP 2: Next, retrieve the short rope. It goes on top of the long piece, slanted from lower right to upper left (fig. 2). You now have an "X" in your hand.

★

STEP 3: This step takes place as you retrieve the medium piece of rope. You move your left middle, ring, and pinkie fingers under and then on top

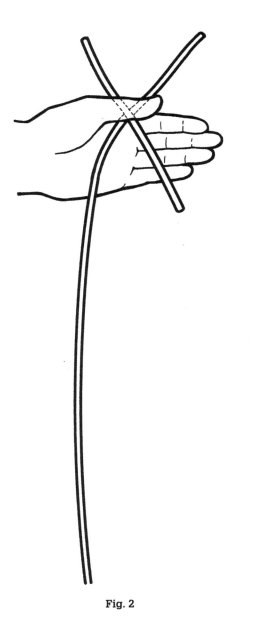

Fig. 2

Reverend Gilbert Stones

After leaving the Fuller Theological Seminary in Pasadena, California, the Reverend Gilbert Stones's first appointment was at the Church of the Good Shepherd, in Kearny, Arizona, almost ninety miles from Tucson. Magic helped him fill the hours that were not devoted to his congregants. Today, at the Woodland Hills United Methodist Church in Los Angeles, where he is the spiritual leader, he uses magic in some of his sermons to get his congregants' attention. His handlebar mustache and Van Dyke beard help set the proper atmosphere for his prestidigitation.

For the past ten years the Reverend Stones has been active in the California magic community. He is a member of the Magic Castle, a Los Angeles magic club, which presents shows and lectures throughout the year for members and their guests.

of the bottom half of the short rope (figs. 3 and 4). This clips the bottom half of the short rope between your index and middle fingers. Next, your thumb goes behind the top of the long piece of rope and kicks it downward (figs. 5 and 6). Last, your index finger goes back under the piece of rope it is on top of. Your thumb holds the interlocked portion against your hand (figs. 7 and 8). This whole step takes about half a second.

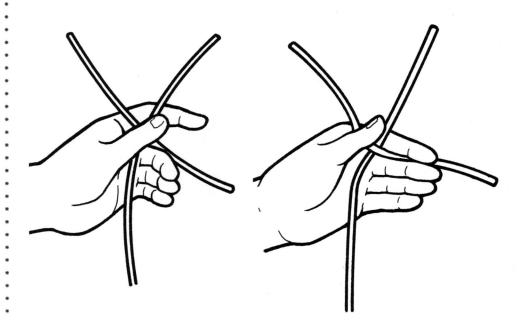

Fig. 3   Fig. 4

Fig. 5   Fig. 6

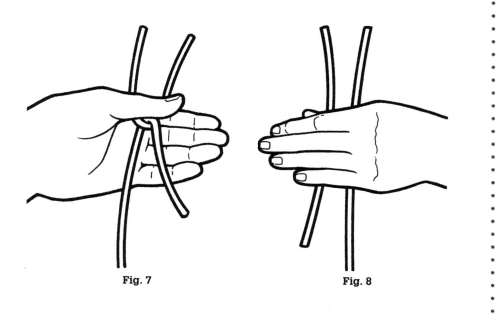

Fig. 7   Fig. 8

★

STEP 4: During step 3, you should have retrieved the medium portion of rope with your right hand. Place it in your left hand, to the right of everything else. Now, close your hand into a fist and release your thumb.

★

STEP 5: It will have appeared as if you have merely placed the ropes in your left hand. With your right hand, gather up the apparent bottoms of the ropes (fig. 9).

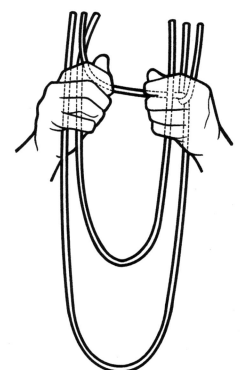

Fig. 9

★

STEP 6: This is the easiest part. Make sure you don't have a vise grip on the ropes in your left hand. (Hold them somewhat loosely, but still make sure you have a good grip on them.) Simply pull to the right with your right hand, and you will see that the ropes have apparently stretched— all are of equal length. Now let go with your right hand, letting the ends dangle from your left hand.

★

STEP 7: For the next few steps, we will label the top ends of the rope, from the magician's left to right, A, B, and C. What you will now do is open your left fingers, at the same time putting your thumb against the ropes. However, make sure your thumb is above the interlocked section. (Fig. 10 is a magician's view, fig. 11 is an audience view.) The following

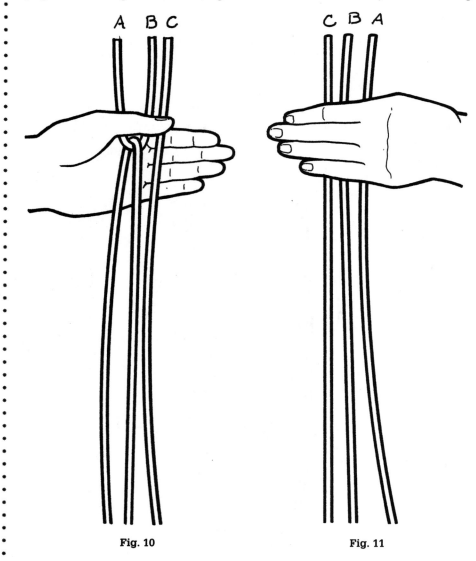

Fig. 10   **Fig. 11**

three steps do not have to be performed, yet I always use them because they are a convincing display of three equal lengths of rope. But they are difficult. So for those readers who do not feel the following display is necessary, go right ahead to step 10.

★

STEP 8: Approach your left hand with your right. You are going to take the single rope (C) and pull it up and out of the hand (fig. 12). Display it. Come back to your left hand with your right, and place the single rope back in your left hand. In a flowing motion, pull up and out of the hand the interlocked portion of A and B with your right hand, and hold onto C with your left (fig. 13). It will appear as if you counted the first rope, and now have added one rope to it, counting two. Whatever you do, make sure the interlocked portion is not seen by the audience.

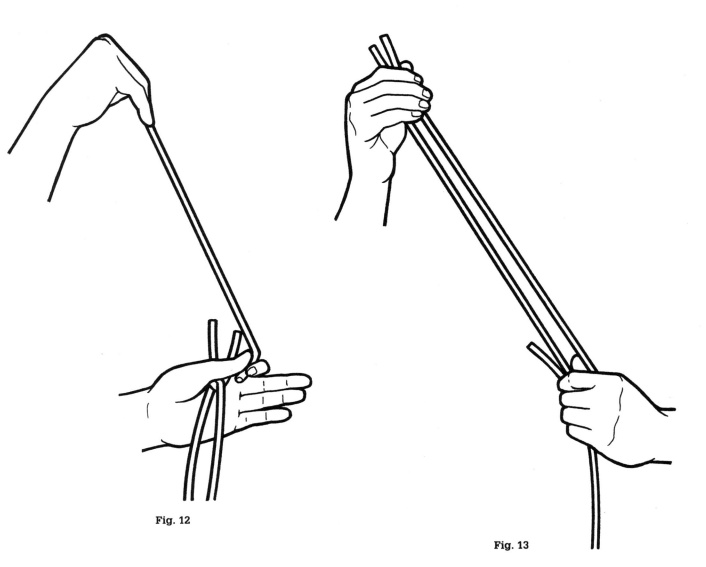

Fig. 12

Fig. 13

★

STEP 9: Display the two ropes in your right hand for a few moments, and finally add the last rope in your left hand to the two in your right, displaying all three ropes. Now transfer all of the ropes in your right hand back into your left.

★

STEP 10: Pause and accept your applause. Now, take the rope that is all the way to the left, the single, individual rope, and sling it over your shoulder with your right hand.

★

STEP 11: You now have what appear to be two equal pieces of rope in your left hand. There should be two ends sticking out above the top of your left hand. These are in reality the two ends of the short rope. What you need to do is tie them together in a single knot. The audience will believe you have tied the two ropes together, but really you have tied the short piece *around* the long piece.

★

STEP 12: Display this long, knotted rope, which appears to be in two equal parts, once again convincing the audience that you have three equal pieces of rope. Finally, take the rope that is slung over your shoulder and tie it to the upper end of the long, knotted rope. You now have one very long rope with two knots in it. The lower knot is actually the short piece.

★

STEP 13: Grip the top end of the rope with your left hand. Now, somewhere in the middle of the rope, grip it with your right hand. Begin to wrap the rope around your left hand. When your right hand hits the lower knot, hold onto that knot, as it will slide (fig. 14). Hold onto it until it has slid to a position about six inches above the bottom end of the rope. Let go of the knot at this juncture. Finish wrapping the rope around your hand. The audience should not know that any deception has taken place.

★

STEP 14: Snap your fingers and unravel the rope, displaying the same knotted rope, yet having a short piece, a long piece, and a medium piece. Untie the knot that separates the medium piece from the long piece, and

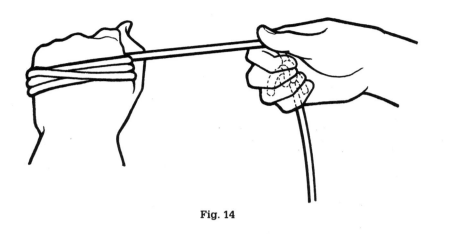

Fig. 14

toss the medium piece into the audience. Now untie the knot that *is* the short piece. Just untie it and display the two ropes. No one will realize that the knot was the short piece. Toss both into the audience and accept your applause.

Selective Timeline of the History of Magic

26th Century B.C. Dedi the magician of Ded-Snefru decapitates and then reunites a goose in a performance for King Cheops of Egypt.

25th Century B.C. Hieroglyphic of conjurers doing cups and balls is drawn in the Beni Hassan tomb in Egypt.

6th Century B.C. First metal coins are minted in Lydia.

5th Century B.C. Ancient Greeks build "Deus Ex Machina," or "God from a Machine." These secretly controlled mechanisms could create noise and move objects to convince people that gods were exerting their mysterious powers.

3rd Century A.D. Greek writer and philosopher Alciphron writes of a magician doing the cups and balls.

4th Century A.D. Hero of Alexandria would make temple doors open as if gods were walking through.

11th Century A.D. King Arthur is tutored by the legendary magician Merlin. Although no one is sure he ever existed, according to believers, Merlin's greatest feat of magic was moving Stonehenge from the Irish countryside to Salisbury Plains, England.

ca. 1445 The Master of Playing Cards, in Basel, Switzerland, engraves the first pictorial deck of cards.

1472 A picture of people at play with cards is found in Ingold's *Das Guildan Spiel* (German book).

1584 Publication of the first known book in English discussing the ways of magicians and perhaps the first book on magic ever, *The Discouerie of Witchcrafte*, by Reginald Scot.

1611 Shakespeare writes in *The Tempest:* "If this be magic, let it be art!"

1612 *The Art of Juggling*, containing one magic trick, written by Samuel Ridd, is the second book explaining the how-to's of magic.

1634 *Hocus Pocus Jr.: The Anatomie of Legerdemain* is published. Though not a teaching text, it is the first book in English (and possibly in any language) *solely devoted* to magic.

1674 Mathew Buchinger, the early conjurer with no hands or legs, is born. Buchinger died in 1722.

1722 The first teaching book solely devoted to magic, *The Whole Art of Legerdemain*, is written by Henry Dean.

1731 Prominent eighteenth-century English magician Isaac Fawkes dies. His birth year is unknown.

1734 In this year we find the first American advertisement for a magician, German-born Joseph Broome, in the *New York Weekly Journal*.

1734 Jacob Meyer, or Jacob Philadelphia as he would later be called, is born in the place that inspired his change of name, Philadelphia. Meyer was probably the first American-born professional magician.

1760 Magician Eliaser Bamberg is born in Holland. Eliaser's son, grandson, great-grandson, and great-great-grandson would all become magicians. This was the first family dynasty of magic. Theo Bamberg, better known as Okito, was Eliaser's great-grandson and the most famous member of the dynasty. Theo's son David was the famous Fu Manchu.

1780 Chevalier Giovanni Guiseppe Pinetti was the first magician to advertise his use of playing cards.

1783 Richard Potter, the first American-born magician to have a successful career in the United States, is born. Potter was the son of a colonial aristocrat and a black slave. His act, titled "Evening's Brush to Sweep Away Care," was often performed by magician Robert Olson as a tribute to Potter in the colonial Old Sturbridge Village in Massachusetts. Potter died in 1835.

1805 Born in Blois, France, French magician Jean Eugene Robert-Houdin is known as the "Father of Modern Magic." This title was given to him because of the many ways he changed magic to keep it current with an ever-changing society. A clock-maker by trade, Robert-Houdin eventually got interested in magic. Perhaps his most famous exploit took place in 1856, the year of a rebellion in Algeria, then a French colony. Apparently, local magicians/priests known as Marabouts had incited certain Arab tribes to revolt. They had been showing the natives that they had much more power than the government by doing magic. At the invitation of the French government, Robert-Houdin traveled to Algeria. At a performance in Algiers attended by a number of important Arab chieftains, he apparently removed the strength of the strongest Marabout in the audience. Other magic effects that Robert-Houdin performed that same night included catching a bullet in an apple and making an audience member disappear. The chieftains were no longer as fascinated with the Marabouts, and the rebels lost the support they needed to continue. Robert-Houdin was credited with putting down the insurrection. Robert-Houdin died in 1871.

1806 The "Beethoven of Magic" and pioneer of card magic, Johann Nepomuk Hofsinzer, is born in Vienna. Hofsinzer called card magic "the poetry of magic." Hofsinzer died in 1875.

1814 John Henry Anderson, "The Great Wizard of the North," is born. Anderson would be the first magician to travel to all of the world's continents. Anderson would also popularize and make an icon of pulling a rabbit out of a hat. Anderson died in 1874.

1843 "Herrmann the Great," Alexander Herrmann, is born. Herrmann was one of the pioneers of close-up magic. He died in 1896.

1849 Harry Kellar, later to be called "The World's Greatest Magician," is born. He popularized the classic illusion, the "Spirit Cabinet." Kellar died in 1922.

1853 Adelaide Herrmann is born Adelaide Scarcez in London. She later married Alexander Herrmann. After Mr. Herrmann died in 1896, Ms. Herrmann kept the show on the road for many years. Some say that she was one of the most outstanding performers of magic to appear on the stage. Adelaide Herrmann died in 1932.

1861 Chung Ling Soo is born William Robinson. Robinson was famous for performing the death-defying bullet catch. Ironically, Robinson was fatally shot while performing the bullet catch trick in 1918.

1867 Thomas Nelson Downs, "The King of Koins," is born. He would write the influential magic book *The Art of Magic* in 1908. Downs is the creator of the classic, oft-imitated coin production act, the "Miser's Dream." T. Nelson Downs died in 1938.

1869 Howard Thurston, later to receive the "Mantle of Magic" along with the title "World's Greatest Magician" from Harry Kellar, is born. Thurston died in 1936.

1873 Max Malini, "The Last of the Mountebanks," is born either Max Katz or Max Katz-Breit. Malini will become one of the most influential and talented magicians of the twentieth century. Among his most important contributions to the art was his streamlining and renewing of the ancient cups and balls trick. Max Malini died in 1942.

1874 Harry Houdini, to become perhaps the most famous magician ever, is born Ehrich Weiss in Hungary. Houdini would go on to become a great escape artist and magician. Houdini died in 1926.

1874 "Carter the Great," Charles Joseph Carter, is born. Carter put himself through college as a magician, billing himself as "Master Charles Carter, America's Youngest Prestidigitator." Carter died in 1936.

1882 Dante/The Great Jansen is born Harry Jansen. Dante would go on to produce and star in one of the most famous touring magic shows, "Sim Sala Bim." Dante died in 1955.

1885 Harry Blackstone, Sr., is born Harry Boughton. Blackstone would become one of the major magicians of the twentieth century. He would gain a reputation for doing such tricks as the floating lightbulb, the floating handkerchief, and recreating the jadoo wallah's Indian rope trick. Blackstone died in 1965. His son, Harry Blackstone, Jr., carries on his legacy.

1894 Dai Vernon, "The Professor," is born David Frederick Wingfield Verner in Canada. Author of many books on magic, creator of innumerable tricks, and widely recognized as an influential teacher of magic, Vernon is generally considered to have been the greatest contributor to the art of close-up magic. Dai Vernon died in 1992 at the age of ninety-eight.

1895 Joseph Dunninger, master mentalist, is born. Dunninger would be one of the first magicians to use broadcast media to its full extent as an advertising power and publicity vehicle. Dunninger died in 1975.

1896 Susy Wandas is born Susy Van Dyke. Susy and her mother later formed an act called The Wandas Sisters, Queens of Magic. Wandas was one of the top women magicians.

1902 The mysterious S. W. Erdnase writes probably the most important book on card technique, *The Expert at the Card Table.* This book, still in print, continues to be used as a text by card gamblers and magicians.

1902 Dell O'Dell, the "Queen of Magic," is born Nell Newton. After her vaudeville career ended, she was host of a children's television show and also owned her own magic shop in California. O'Dell died in 1962.

1920 Another icon of magic, sawing a woman in half, is created by Percy Tibbles, whose stage name was P. T. Selbit. Horace Goldin of New York later improved the trick by making the subject's head, feet, and hands stick out of the box.

1926 Dr. Harlan Tarbell begins compiling his *Tarbell Course in Magic,* a detailed set of instructions and commentary which eventually was to cover virtually every aspect of the art of magic. Dr. Tarbell himself provided the illustrations supporting his text.

1938 *Greater Magic* is published by Carl Waring Jones Publishing. Written by John Northern Hilliard, this is probably the most complete single volume on magic ever written.

1941 Louis Tannen, Inc., publishes the first book of the original six comprising the *Tarbell Course in Magic*. The *Tarbell Course* is generally considered the magician's bible. Since Tarbell's death, two more volumes have been penned, one by Harry Lorayne, and one by Richard Kaufman.

1947 Doug Henning is born in Manitoba, Winnipeg. Henning would bring magic to a new, high level of popularity. Henning would have three Broadway shows and several national TV specials. Henning presented to audiences a strikingly different look and sound than the public was accustomed to. His shoulder-length hair, drooping mustache, and dazzling smile instantly caught the audience's attention. No white tie, tails, and top hat for Henning. Rather, bright-colored leotards and rock and roll music struck a responsive chord in his audiences.

1957 David Copperfield is born David Kotkin in Metuchen, New Jersey. Copperfield has the record for the most television specials, and probably has greater name recognition than any other magician in the twentieth century with the possible exception of Harry Houdini.

1974 Doug Henning's first Broadway show, *The Magic Show*, opens on May 28. It is a huge success and runs for four years.

1977 David Copperfield has his first TV special on ABC. The first of his annual specials appears on CBS the next year.

1977 Kaufman & Greenberg, publishers of magic books, is founded by two magicians, writer/illustrator Richard Kaufman and banker Alan C. "Ace" Greenberg. By 1995 it had published forty-four books on magic, more than any other publisher at the time.

1994 Magician Ricky Jay has a hit one-man show, *Ricky Jay and His 52 Assistants*. The show sold out its entire run on the first day tickets were sold.

1996 Magic is at an all-time high level of popularity. David Copperfield will have had twenty television specials, starting with his first, in 1977, all with top ratings. Magic on television, however, is not restricted to Copperfield. In the month of May 1996 alone, there were no less than six magic television specials on the major TV networks—CBS, NBC, ABC, and Fox. Regular relevision shows like *Lois and Clark*, *Wings*, *Burke's Law*, *Star Trek: Deep Space Nine*, *The Simpsons*, *Nash Bridges*, and many others have all presented magic in one or more of their episodes. Outside of television, magic is happening everywhere. At least six CD-ROMs about magic have been released; a lecture series about magic was featured at the Smithsonian Institution; and a large, magic-themed restaurant called *Magic Underground* is scheduled to open in New York. The *New York Times,* the *Los Angeles Times,* and even *Playboy* have all had lengthy articles about magic or magicians. Movies, including the record-breaking *Mission: Impossible* have included footage on magic or sleight of hand. People throughout the world pay hundreds of millions of dollars every year to see magic performed. It looks like the art of magic might just be here to stay.

Magic Stores Throughout the United States

Bert Easley's Fun Shop
509 West McDowell Road
Phoenix, Arizona 85003
602-271-9146

Williams Magic & Novelties
6528 East 22nd Street
Tucson, Arizona 85710
602-790-4060

Hollywood Magic, Inc.
6614 Hollywood Blvd.
Hollywood, California 90028
213-464-5610

Owen Magic Supreme
734 N. McKeever Avenue
Azusa, California 91702
818-969-4519

House of Magic
2025 Chestnut Street
San Francisco, California 94123
415-346-2218

Winkler's Warehouse of Wonders
24 Doyle Road
Oakdale, Connecticut 06370
203-859-3474

Al's Magic Shop
1012 Vermont Avenue NW
Washington, D.C. 20005
202-789-2800

Daytona Magic*
136 S. Beach Street
Daytona Beach, Florida 32114
800-346-2442

*If none of the stores on this list are in your area, either look in the Yellow Pages or contact one of the five asterisked stores, all of which conduct a significant mail order business.

More Than Balloons
2409 Ravendale
Kissimmee, Florida 34758-2213
407-933-8888

Magic, Inc.
5082 N. Lincoln Avenue
Chicago, Illinois 60625
312-334-2855

Magic Attic at Union Station
39 Jackson Place
Indianapolis, Indiana 46225
317-635-1550

Stevens Magic Emporium*
2520 East Douglas
Wichita, Kansas 67214
316-683-9582

Hank Lee's Magic Factory*
127 South Street
Boston, Massachusetts 02111
617-482-8749

Ken-Zo's Magic Studio
1025 So. Charles Street
Baltimore, Maryland 21230
410-727-5811

Abbott's Magic Co.*
124 St. Joseph
Colon, Michigan 49040
616-432-3235

Geno Munari's Magic Shop
3799 Las Vegas Blvd.
So. Las Vegas, Nevada 89109
702-736-2883

Mecca Magic, Inc.
49 Dodd Street
Bloomfield, New Jersey 07003
201-429-7597

Flosso/Hornmann Magic Shop
45 West 34th Street
New York, New York 10001
212-279-6079

Louis Tannen, Inc.*
24 West 25th Street
New York, New York 10010
212-929-4500

Guaranteed Magic
27 Bright Road
Hatboro, Pennsylvania 19040
215-672-3344

Collector's Workshop
38427 Snickersville Tpke.
Middleburg, Virginia 22117
540-687-6476

Magic Tricks
101 14th Street N.W.
Charlottesville, Virginia 22903
804-293-5788

Market Magic
1501 Pike Place #427
Seattle, Washington 98101
206-624-4271

Bibliography

Allen, Stan, ed. "Inside Magic," *Magic* (June 1993–July 1995).

Bech, Leonard. "Things Magical in the Collections of the Rare Book Division." *Quarterly Journal of the Library of Congress* (October 1974).

Bengel, Robert. *Getting Back to Basics*. N.p.: Self-published, 1992.

Blackstone, Harry, Jr. *The Blackstone Book of Magic and Illusion*. New York: Newmarket Press, 1985.

Booth, John N. "Memoirs of a Magician's Ghost." *Linking Ring* (1963–1995).

Cassidy, John, and Michael Stroud. *The Klutz Book of Magic*. Palo Alto, Calif.: Klutz Press, 1990.

Christopher, Milbourne. *The Illustrated History of Magic*. New York: Crowell, 1973.

———. *Panorama of Magic*. New York: Dover, 1962.

———. *Panorama of Prestidigitators*. New York: Privately published, 1956.

Clarke, Sidney W. *The Annals of Conjuring*. New York: Magico Magazine Reprint, 1983.

Dawes, Edwin A. *The Great Illusionists*. New York: Chartwell Books, 1979.

———. "A Rich Cabinet of Magical Curiosities." *Magic Circular* (May 1972–95).

Fischer, Ottokar. *Illustrated Magic*. New York: Macmillan, 1943.

Gibson, Walter B. *Houdini's Fabulous Magic*. New York: Crown, 1961.

———. *The Master Magicians*. New York: Doubleday, 1966.

———. *The Original Houdini Scrapbook*. New York: Corwin Sterling, 1976.

Gibson, Walter B., and Morris N. Young. *Houdini on Magic*. New York: Dover, 1953.

Gresham, William Lindsay. *Houdini: The Man Who Walked Through Walls*. Winter Park, Fla.: Macfadden.

Henning, Doug, with Charles Reynolds. *Houdini: His Legend and His Magic*. New York: New York Times Books, 1977.

Hilliard, John Northern. *Greater Magic*. Minneapolis: Carl Waring Jones Publications, 1938.

James, Stewart. *Abbott's Encyclopedia of Rope Tricks*. Colon, Mich.: Abbott's Magic Novelty Co.

Jay, Ricky. *Learned Pigs and Fireproof Women*. New York: Villard Books, 1986.

Larsen, Erika. "Genii News." *Genii* (December 1991–May 1995).

Levine, Michael. *The Address Book*. New York: Berkley Publishing Group, 1995.

Lewis, Angelo (Professor Hoffman). *Modern Magic*. Cheshire, Conn.: Magic Book Club/Biblo.

Lorayne, Harry. *Close-Up Card Magic*. New York: Louis Tannen, 1962.

———. *The Tarbell Course in Magic, vol. 7*. New York: Louis Tannen, 1972.

Marx, Harpo, with Rowland Barber. *Harpo Speaks*. London: Victor Gollancz, 1961.

Minch, Stephen and John Carney. *Carneycopia*. Tahoma, Calif.: L & L Publishing, 1991.

Moulton, H. J., and Milbourne Christopher. *Houdini's History of Magic in Boston, 1792–1915*. Glenwood, Ill.: Meyerbooks, 1983.

Mulholland, John. *The Early Magic Shows*. New York: Privately published by the Office of John Mulholland, 1945.

———. "The Hand Is Not Quicker Than the Eye." *New York Times Magazine,* October 8, 1933, pp. 9, 17.

———. *Quicker Than the Eye.* Indianapolis: Self-published, 1932.

Ortiz, Darwin. *The Annotated Erdnase.* Pasadena, Calif: Magical Publications, 1991.

Pecor, Charles. *The Magician on the American Stage, 1752–1874.* Washington, D.C.: Emerson & West Publishing, 1977.

Perlmutter, Alvin H., Executive Producer. *The Illusion of News.* Hosted by Bill Moyers, Public Affairs Television, Inc., WNET New York; WETA, Washington, D.C., 1989.

Potter, Jack. *The Master Index to Magic in Print.* Vols. 1–14. Alberta, Canada: Mickey Hades International Enterprises, 1967–68.

Price, David. *Magic: A Pictorial History of Conjurers in the Theater.* Toronto: Cornwall Books, 1985.

Rauscher, William V. *John Calvert: Magic and Adventures Around the World.* Baton Rouge: Claitor's Publishers, 1989.

Rich, Frank. "To Play Oneself May Be the Greatest Illusion of All." *New York Times,* June 29, 1986, Arts & Leisure Section, pp. 3 and 25.

Robinson, Ben, with Larry White. *Twelve Have Died.* Watertown, Mass.: Ray Goulet's Magic Art Book Co., 1986.

Roth, David, with Richard Kaufman. *David Roth's Expert Coin Magic.* N.p.: Kaufman and Greenberg, 1985.

Scarne, John. *The Odds Against Me.* New York: Simon and Schuster, 1966.

Sharpe, S. H. *Neo Magic.* London: George Johnson Magical Publications, 1932.

Siegel, Lee. *Net of Magic.* Chicago: University of Chicago Press, 1991.

Starke, George. *Stars of Magic.* New York: D. Robbins & Co.,1975.

Tarbell, Harlan. *The Tarbell Course in Magic.* 6 vols. New York: Louis Tannen Publishers, 1941–54.

———, with Richard Kaufman and Steve Burton. *The Tarbell Course in Magic, vol. 8.* New York: D. Robbins & Co., 1993.

Tarr, Bill. *Now You See It, Now You Don't.* New York: Vintage Books, 1976.

Wilson, Mark, with Walter Gibson. *The Mark Wilson Complete Course in Magic.* N. Hollywood, Calif.: Courage Books, 1988.

ndex